CROSSCURRENTS IN

AMERICAN

IMPRESSIONISM

AT THE TURN

OF THE CENTURY

American Impressionism

AT THE TURN

OF THE CENTURY

William U. Eiland

GENERAL EDITOR

Donald Keyes

Janice Simon

EDITORS

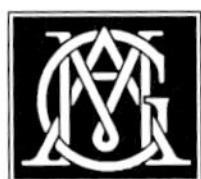

Cover: John Henry Twatchman
Court of Honor, World's Columbian Exposition, Chicago, 1893
Oil on canvas
25 x 30 inches
Bequest of Frederick W. Schumacher, 1957
Columbus Museum of Art, Ohio

Crosscurrents in American Impressionism at the Turn of the Century
Design: Erin Kirk New
Production: Lazzari Graphics
Typeface: Minion
Department of Publications: Bonnie Ramsey, Jennifer DePrima and Laura Mullins
Printed in an edition of 1000 by University Printing,
University of Georgia

Library of Congress No. 93-1745
ISBN 0-915977-16-8

Library of Congress Cataloging-in-Publication Data

Crosscurrents in American Impressionism art at the turn of the century
    / William U. Eiland, general editor, Donald D. Keyes and Janice Simon, editors.
        p.   cm.
        Includes bibliographical references.
        ISBN 0-915977-16-8
        1. Impressionism (Art)—United States. 2. Painting, American. 3. Painting, Modern—
        19th century—United States. 4. Painting, Modern—20th century—United States.
        I. Eiland, William U. II. Keyes, Donald D. III. Simon, Janice.
    ND210.5.I4C76 1995
    759.13'09'034—dc20   95-1745
                                                                            CIP

This project is supported in part by the Georgia Council for the Arts through the
appropriations of the Georgia General Assembly through the National Endowment for the Arts.
A portion of the museum's operating support has been provided by the Institute of Museum
Services, a federal agency that offers general operating support to the nation's museums.
Individuals, foundations, and corporations provide additional museum support through
their gifts to the University of Georgia Foundation. The assistance of the Offices of the
Vice-Presidents for Research and Academic Affairs at the University of Georgia made this
project possible.

CONTENTS

ACKNOWLEDGEMENTS

THIS VOLUME IS THE SECOND in a series devoted to issues in the history of art. The Georgia Museum of Art holds annual symposia at which scholars are invited to present original research related to special exhibitions. The first volume in this series, *The Craft of Art: Industry and Originality in the Italian Renaissance and Baroque Workshop*, published by the University of Georgia Press in 1995, was the result of a series of lectures held in conjunction with the exhibition *Artists and Artisans of Florence: Works from the Horne Museum* at the museum from September 16 to November 22, 1992. The articles in *Crosscurrents in American Impressionism at the Turn of the Century* were delivered as public lectures accompanying the exhibition *American Impressionism in Georgia Collections* at the museum from September 11 to November 14, 1993. The third volume, now in production and scheduled to appear in 1996, will publish articles by four scholars on images of women and peasants in seventeenth-century Dutch art as a complement to the museum's exhibition and catalogue *Adriaen Van Ostade: Etchings of Peasant Life in Holland's Golden Age* held in 1994.

In the belief that each volume contains significant research that we are happy to make available to a wider audience, both academic and lay, we are grateful to the scholars whose articles appear in this book. In addition, Donald Keyes, the exhibition's curator, and Janice Simon, associate professor of art history at the University of Georgia and a contributor, are due thanks for editing this collection. The staff of the museum, in particular the members of the registrar's department and the preparators, worked hard to assure the success of the exhibition, one of the best-attended in the museum's history. Stephanie Kaplan also provided invaluable services to this project. Without the astute attention and careful work of Bonnie Ramsey and her staff, in particular the diligent and patient efforts of Jennifer DePrima, Meg Pearson, Laura Mullins, and students working in the department of publications, neither the catalogue nor the current volume would have been possible. Finally, we would not be able to continue this series without the financial assistance of the offices of the vice-presidents for research and for academic affairs at the University of Georgia.

Acknowledgements

The staff of the museum join me in thanking Jack and Jeffie Rowland and Dr. and Mrs. Tom Cooper for partial funding of the exhibition itself.

WILLIAM U. EILAND
General Editor and Director of the Georgia Museum of Art

INTRODUCTION

AROUND THE TURN OF THE CENTURY, and certainly prior to World War I, American Impressionism had become the national style and indeed a world-wide phenomenon, at least in the Western world. During the last twenty years it might seem as though Impressionism triumphantly entered America and rolled from New York and Boston through Chicago to San Francisco and San Diego without a murmur of dissent or doubt. Nothing could be further from the truth, as evidenced by the essays in this volume.

What viewers in the late twentieth century see as Impressionism's beauty and charm, many at the turn of the century cited as vapid decoration, unskilled non-art, and even insidiousness. One reason for the mistaken notion of the style's popularity is the history, often propounded in art-historical texts, of the linear evolution of Occidental art from French Romantic painting and British Naturalism to the Barbizon School and French Realism, Impressionism and Post Impressionism, and the triumph of modernism in Paris prior to World War I. As distorted as this history might be, from the American viewpoint it is even further from the truth.

As scholars such as Robert Weibe have noted, the period from 1880 to 1920 was dominated by a search for order in a country seemingly in chaos. From the assassination of two presidents in a little over thirty years to the devastating labor strikes across the land, the United States appeared to be tearing itself apart. Values that had seemed immutable only a generation before were regularly abrogated by well-meaning people. No area of American life was safe from revision, witness the growing acceptance of Darwinism and the women's suffrage movement. New inventions, including the automobile, the phonograph, and moving pictures; new sciences, including psychoanalysis and atomic physics; and new modes of living, such as apartment houses and federal income taxes, challenged every American. Ranging from literature to music, architecture to dance, all forms of art concurrently underwent dramatic changes. Theodore Dreiser, Charles Ives, Frank Lloyd Wright, and Isadora Duncan are among the best known participants in this upheaval.

The visual arts in America did not speak with one voice during this period as they had during the first two-thirds of the century. Indeed, it was more like a cacophony. In the mid-1880s, at the same time that French Impressionism first reached these shores, the Vanderbilts were building their "cottages" in Newport, and the Metropolitan Museum of Art, hardly a decade old, was competing with the new stores on Ladies' Mile by training students in the finer points of plumbing. Until the end of World War I in 1918, there existed in American art a profusion of divergent, often conflicting styles and aesthetics: Neo-Renaissance, Arts and Crafts, Tonalism, romantic academicism, Realism, Impressionism, Post Impressionism, and modernism.

American Impressionism reflected the diversity and contradictions found in the other arts at the turn of the century. Assuming the core of American Impressionism can be identified by The Ten, the New York and Boston painters who assembled in 1898 and exhibited continuously until 1919 under the rubric of Impressionism, then why was Winslow Homer, the well-known proponent of Realism, invited to be a member? Many in the group, such as John Twatchtman, tended to utilize a style that embraced a modified Tonalism. Painters who used an impressionistic style included members of The Eight, such as William Glackens, supposedly from the enemy camp of the Realists, the "Apostles of Ugliness." Last, the crowning of the movement as America's national style in 1915 at the Panama Pacific International Exposition in San Francisco occurred two years after the notorious Armory Show in New York City and the initial assault of the modernists.

The five essays that follow derive from lectures given during the presentation of the exhibition *American Impressionism in Georgia Collections*, which opened at the Georgia Museum of Art in 1993. The authors have looked at the artists and their work in detail, eschewing popular notions of American Impressionism. As a result, the five scholars give the reader an innovative and rich understanding of the movement. This follows my intentions for the exhibition, which presented a selection of artists from across the country working in a wide variety of Impressionist styles.

I am in debt to the authors, whose patience during the editing process has made this a far better scholarly document. Janice Simon, associate professor of art history at the University of Georgia, has not only written an insightful essay but has also edited all the other essays. To her I owe a great debt of thanks. Stephanie Kaplan, assistant registrar at the Georgia Museum of Art, has skillfully undertaken the laborious task of finding the photographs for the illustrations and making sure permission was granted for their use.

DONALD. D. KEYES
Curator of Paintings

CROSSCURRENTS IN AMERICAN IMPRESSIONISM AT THE TURN OF THE CENTURY

The Promise of 1893

JANICE SIMON

The fog arose suddenly after a glorious morning of blue sky and sunlight. A north fog, cold and gray, enveloping Chicago, then the suburbs, then the extraordinary group of buildings which the popular fancy has so aptly termed "The White City." All white they had been that morning, the morning of my farewell; white as a marble town outlined against a sky untarnished as themselves. How they stood out, still white, in the dense enshrouding fog; but it was the whiteness of a phantom village, whose contours were merged in mist, whose domes, colonnades and towers lost all solidity—a dreamy vision of architecture, vague scenery about a phantom crowd. They were no longer men whom I saw coming and going, but moving spots, forms so well obliterated that the hum of voices escaping that crowd, confused and muffled by the fog, became the faintest murmur. . . In the last glance I gave that fading, shifting panorama, it seemed to me, that chancing there that autumn day, first clear, then veiled, I had experienced in a few short hours the extremes of that city's fascination: first, its dazzling brilliancy, then its fading gloom, all of which would give it legendary charm. I had realized the melancholy touch which every human masterpiece requires to make it truly beautiful—effacement in the past.

PAUL BOURGET, "A Farewell to the White City," *The Cosmopolitan*, 1893

IRONICALLY, FRENCHMAN PAUL BOURGET articulated perhaps better than any contemporary native writer the essence of America's greatest cultural and ideological production of the *fin de siècle*—the World's Columbian Exposition. Intended to surpass France's centennial fair of 1889 and to out-Europe Europe, the Chicago world's fair of 1893 proclaimed America's arrival as a full-fledged civilization as it celebrated the four-hundredth anniversary of Columbus's arrival to the New World. For many a spectator the fair was an ethereal, utopian vision of America in the modern age.

Bourget's impressionistic recollection, full of references to the transitory effects of atmosphere, light, and memory, captures the elusive nature of the fair. At once "a marble town" and "a phantom village," "dazzling" and "fading," "The White City" (as the exposition was known for its Neo-Classical, Beaux-Arts buildings made of white staff) was as contradictory as America and her cultural productions at the turn of the century. Bourget recognized that the "White City's" ideality yet ephemerality distinguished it from the urban realities of the ever-growing "Black City" of Chicago. Indeed, for Bourget that contrast was the source of its greatness and significance. "The White City" was not an end result that fell short of the impressive city surrounding it, as did the expositions held in London and Paris but instead was an inspiring "promise." It heralded the possibility of a superior civilization emerging from a "vast, ingenuous commonwealth, fed unceasingly by heterogeneous elements . . . with its contrasts of extreme refinement and primitive crudity." It offered hope that American democracy could produce not just the utilitarian but also the ideal that is art. Bourget regarded the fair as "an indelible object lesson" in new ideas, as a "prophetic reflection" of the future.[1] Today, the World's Columbian Exposition offers art historians an object lesson in *fin-de-siècle* American culture, society, and its singular conception of Impressionist painting. In particular, it illuminates the culture's fundamental dualities: the urban and the natural, the national and the cosmopolitan, the modern and the academic, the individual and the type, the secular and the sacred, the real and the ideal.[2]

John Twachtman's stunning *Court of Honor, World's Columbian Exposition, Chicago* of 1893 (Fig. 1) embodies all of these contradictory elements. It partakes of the American Impressionist fascination with the fair's ghostly white buildings, Venetian-like waters, and atmospheric, shifting panoramas.[3] Yet it is a prime example of this artist's individualistic assimilation of Impressionist and Tonalist aesthetics to create a transcendental vision. Although Twachtman recorded the impressive architecture and fountains of the fair in *Court of Honor*, he emphasized the natural elements of sky, water, greenery, and light that transformed exposition buildings into the dreamy vision Bourget described so eloquently. An atmospheric haze softens the white Beaux-Arts edifices of the Machinery and Electricity Buildings which housed the premier inventions of urban modernism, the dynamo, and the tower of electricity. The golden-domed Administration Building, at once recalling St. Peter's and the nation's Capitol, shimmers in the center of the court with its yellow and orange-pink coloring. Just as the urban and the natural interweave in a complex dialogue in *Court of Honor*, so too do the academic and the modern. Twachtman modernized the conservative Beaux-Arts facades of his ostensible subject through the Japanese and Chinese aesthetics of a reductive and asymmetrical composition, subtle tonalities, and bold color accents. *Court of Honor* offers a perspective of the stone fence, light poles, and pennants on the right, but counteracts its traditional, spatial effect with extended surfaces of water and sky. A simplified color scheme flattens the scene as well. Orange-pink accents between the columnar

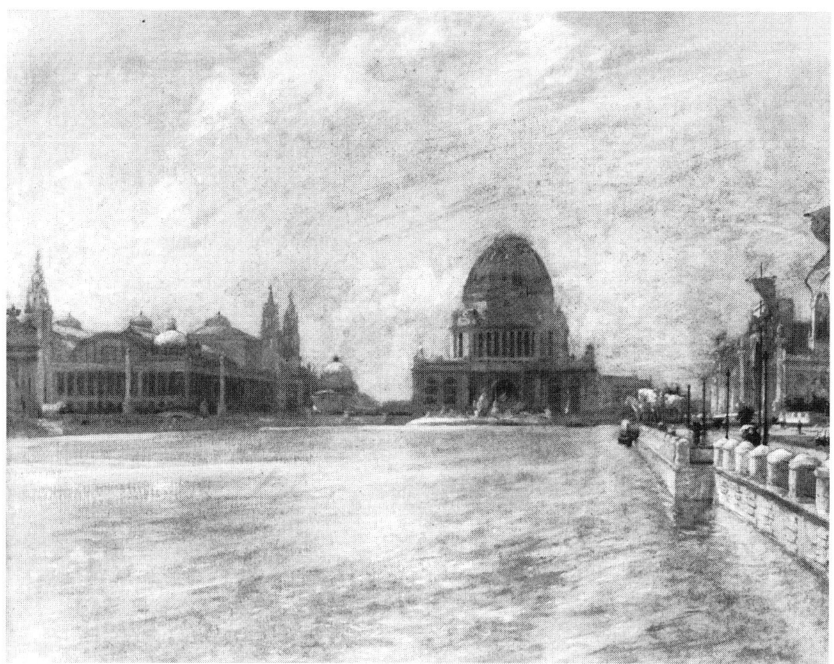

FIGURE 1 John Henry Twachtman, *Court of Honor, World's Columbian Exposition, Chicago*, 1893. Oil on canvas. Columbus Museum of Art, bequest of Frederick W. Schumacher.

grid of the central Administration Building play off the similarly colored pennants with yellow emblems. A touch of green on a kiosk to the left harmonizes with the foliage on the right, and the pink accented dome above the kiosk echoes the Administration Building's grid and the Electricity Building's roof. Thin brushstrokes defining water and sky over a mauve ground activate the painting's surface. Their soft blue-gray tonalities make what at first seems corporeal and fixed hauntingly ethereal and eternal. The descriptive and topographical become aesthetic and spiritual. The Court of Honor is no longer an architectural space merely to be visited, but a mesmerizing cultural vision. It is America's heavenly city, her New Jerusalem.[4] Twachtman's distinctive impressionistic rendition of this seminal, cultural event suggests that indeed the promise of 1893 involved an American formulation of modernism. The nature of that modernism at the turn of the century, epitomized in America's adoption of Impressionism, however, was as complex and contradictory as the World's Columbian Exposition itself.

The World's Columbian Exposition took three years to plan, finance, and construct. Built on the swampland of Jackson Park in the Chicago basin with such impermanent materials as plaster, cement, and jute fibers over iron and timber shed constructions, it succumbed to a series of devasting fires only nine months after it opened to the public in May 1893. A product of both elite and popular culture, the fair was a work of art and an appeal to mass consumption. It simultaneously embraced tradition and progress, the academic and the modern. It was serious and playful, ideal and mundane, reposeful and energetic, ordered and chaotic. It wedded the sacred and the secular, the eternal and the transient, dream and reality.

Such dualities were transparently evident in the layout of the fair which opposed the unified, formal Court of Honor (Fig. 2) with its white academic buildings evoking Classical, Renaissance, and Baroque Europe, to the rambling, eclectic area north of the lagoon with its architecturally diverse state and foreign buildings. Behind the Court of Honor's Beaux-Arts facades that identified America with the highest levels of civilization, the visitor encountered commercial displays of plenitude and invention that announced America as a progressive economic and industrial power.[5]

The Midway Plaisance (Fig. 3), extending westward from the juncture of the Court of Honor and the north lagoon area, provided a stark contrast to the high culture and progressivism of the "White City" proper. As William Dean Howells noted, "in the Fair City, everything is free; in the Plaisance everything must be paid for."[6] For a price, one could ride the Ferris wheel, walk along the streets of Cairo, watch ceremonial dances in the Dahomey village, gawk at the exotic oriental dancer Fatima, and marvel at the Hagenbeck Trained Animal show. In a state of excited anticipation, one reporter alluded to the deliberately chaotic essence of the Midway:

> It will be a jumble of foreignness—a bit of Fez and Nuremberg, of Sahara and Dahomey and Holland, Japan and Rome and Coney Island. It will be gorgeous with color, pulsating with excitement, riotous with the strivings of a battalion of bands, and peculiar to the last degree.[7]

The Midway combined a carnival atmosphere, ethnology, and consumerism. Its exploitative displays of the exotic and the so-called savage created, in the words of contemporary novelist Clara Louisa Burnham, "a mile-long babel. . . [a] representation of matter" that was redeemed as one passed through the Women's Pavillion to the "great, beautiful silence" of the "White City," "an emblem of mind."[8] The Midway world of the primitive Other yielded to the civilization of the "White City." As a peripheral wing to the highly organized and

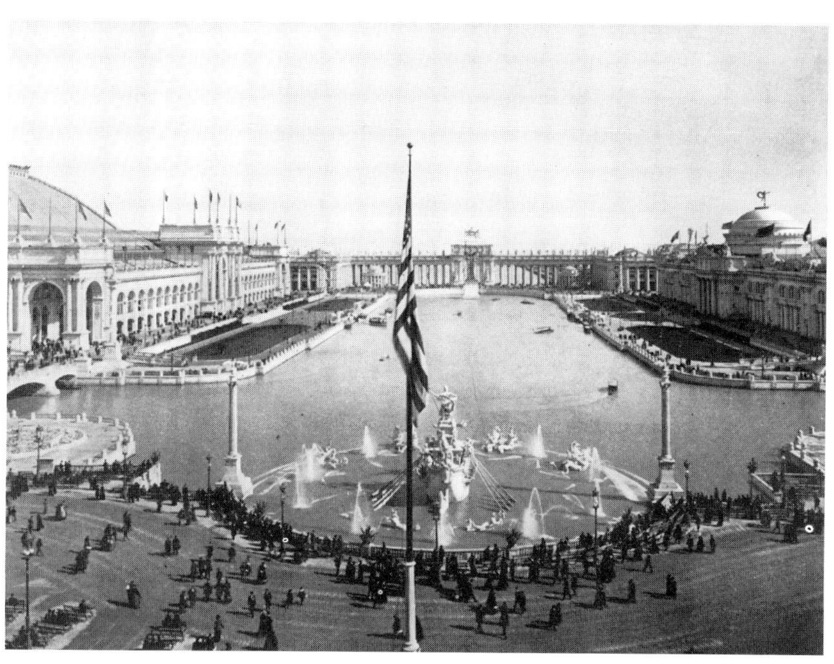

FIGURE 2 *An East View from MacMonnie's Columbian Fountain,* photograph from *The Magic City*, J.W. Buel. Historical Publishing Company, 1894.

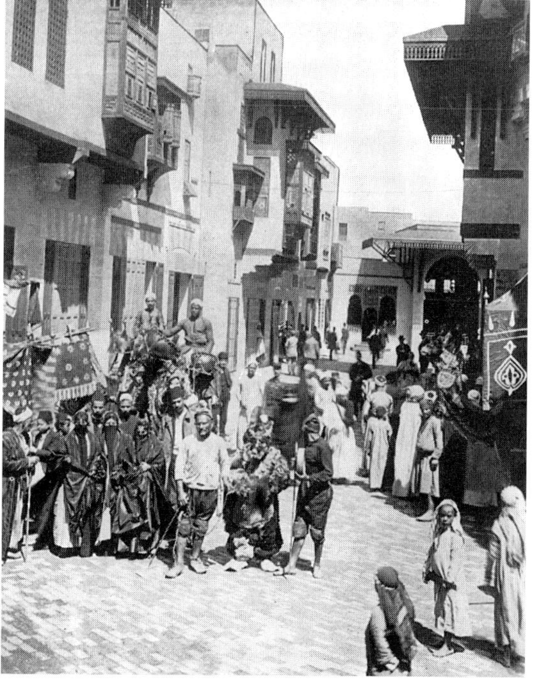

FIGURE 3 *Carnival in the Street of Cairo*, photograph from *The Magic City*, J.W. Buel. Historical Publishing Company, 1894.

contained Court of Honor, the Midway functioned as the lowest rung of the exposition's social evolutionary ladder. George Brown Goode of the Smithsonian Institution voiced just such a conception in his plans for the fair as "an illustrated encyclopedia of humanity," displaying "the steps of progress of civilization and its arts in successive centuries, and in all lands up to the present time." Its organization would "formulate the Modern."[9] The essentially white, middle-class crowd of the exposition with fashionable dress, top hats, and parasols could stare safely at the "turbaned, sandalled, greased, and befeathered inhabitants" hired to entertain them in the Midway Plaisance.[10]

Imperialist in spirit, the World's Columbian Exposition affirmed Anglo-Saxon hegemony and superiority in the face of expanding racial diversity as immigrants crowded the nation's cities. It offered a vision of an ordered, corporate, modern society that seemingly resolved the social tensions of a disaffected world. Six years after the fair, the United States became a significant colonial power with its victory in the Spanish-American War. As if consciously invoking architect Henry Van Brunt's declaration that with the "White City" he wished to prove that "order is heaven's first law," Senator Albert Beveridge proclaimed in 1899 that God "has made us *the* master organizers of the world to establish system where chaos reigns. . . . He has made us adepts in government that we may administer government among savages and senile peoples."[11]

The Art Palace, located north of the lagoon, played its own role in proclaiming the advancement of American civilization. Like the "White City" as a whole, the Art Palace demonstrated what Bourget designated as another lesson of the fair: a democracy could transcend utilitarian needs to create the immortal principle of ideal beauty.[12] E. C. Stedman, one of the architects of the fair, noted, "that to rouse the sense of beauty itself among our faraway plain people was the highest mission of the Fair. It sent thousands back to unlovely homes with the beginning of a noble discontent."[13] During most of the nation's history, Americans distrusted the visual arts and regarded their artistic productions as woefully inadequate in comparison to European achievements. The Chicago fair was to be America's aesthetic coming-out party, a declaration that in the fine arts as in industrial production she had come of age.

Disparities, however, interfered with its success. Organizers intended the American exhibition (Fig. 4), the largest in the Palace, to demonstrate the progress of artists since the Centennial in creating a sophisticated national style. But the exhibition presented more of a Midway-like visual babel of styles and genres. Such academic historical narratives of the Puritan past as Walter McEwen's *The Witches* (c. 1892, private collection) contrasted with such spiritual allegories as Elihu Vedder's *A Soul in Bondage* (1891, The Brooklyn Museum)

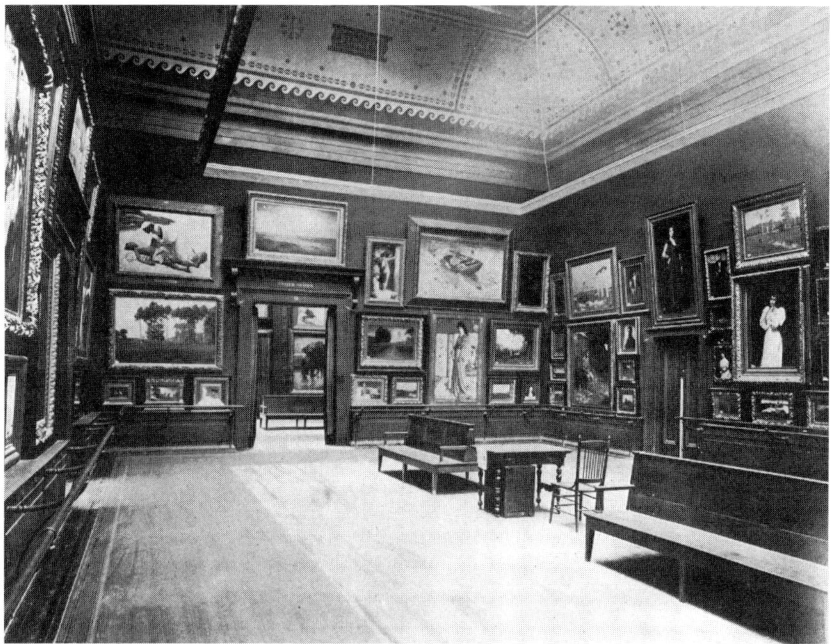

FIGURE 4 *Gallery No. 9 of the United States Section of Painting*, photograph from
The Magic City, J.W. Buel. Historical Publishing Company, 1894.

which in turn offered a strange, symbolist version of Thomas Eakins's haunting
psychological study of despair, *Portrait of a Lady (Amelia Van Buren)* (1889-91,
The Phillips Collection). John George Brown's idealized urban bootblacks,
Winslow Homer's expressive Darwinian marines, Frank Vincent Dumond's de-
tailed religious narratives, and Childe Hassam's impressionistic views of the
streets of Paris confused consensus about the true nature or achievement of
American art. The nation's most innovative artists such as Dwight Tryon,
Thomas Dewing, and Theodore Robinson shared wall space with Hudson River
School holdovers like Worthington Whittredge and stiff academic classicists like
Kenyon Cox. Although the exhibition sought to highlight the nation's artistic
advancement, Thomas Hovenden's stylistically and conceptually conservative
narrative, *Breaking the Home Ties* (1890, Philadelphia Museum of Art), won the
public's highest approval. Women artists were underrepresented even though by
the end of the century their numbers had grown impressively as they made ever
more significant contributions to the profession. American art sold poorly; European sales were ten times more successful.[14]

Just as incongruous elements disturbed the general unity of the Chicago fair, American Impressionism contributed an ironical element to the Art Palace's exhibition. American critics of the *fin de siècle* demanded the formation of a new national art; they found it in an art that had its origins primarily in France. One critic recounted all the areas of France which seemed to crop up in American art, declaring that *that* is where America's national art is to be found. The organizers of the exhibition encouraged such comparisons by placing the American and French displays of nearly comparable size virtually next to one another. A show of foreign art in American collections, including French Impressionist works, linked the two. French art, whether admired or not, became the standard by which American art at the fair was judged.[15] Artists were challenged to create a distinctive and even innovative American voice. The essential question of the Art Palace's exhibition was whether American art, especially American Impressionism, would live up to the promise of 1893.

The World's Columbian Exposition inaugurated Impressionism as an aesthetic force to be reckoned with in American culture. A number of American Impressionists and those artists now associated with Tonalism exhibited at the fair,[16] attracting attention with works that looked quite modern in comparison to the usual American painting such as Hovenden's *Breaking the Home Ties*. Several years later, the Panama-Pacific International Exposition of 1915 held in San Francisco, with its retrospective displays of American Impressionists, signaled Impressionism's full public acceptance to the point that it became a household style. Impressionism, therefore, like the World's Columbian Exposition, participated in America's conception of modernism. Indeed, America adopted European modes of modernism in her *fin-de-siècle* art and expositions; however, she conservatively retreated from a full embrace.

In *The Communist Manifesto* of 1848, Karl Marx envisioned the classic dynamics of the modernist revolution about to transform European culture:

All fixed, fast-frozen relations, with their train of ancient and venerable prejudices and opinions, are swept away, all new-formed ones become antiquated before they can ossify. All that is solid melts into air, all that is holy is profaned, and men at last are forced to face. . .the real conditions of their lives and their relations with their fellow men.[17]

Marx's conception of a world in perpetual revision found its ultimate realization in twentieth-century America. But as *fin-de-siècle* Americans encountered the development of the modern in their physical surroundings and social structures, artists and intellectuals formulated a "reluctant modernism" in response to monumental change. A traditional need for order and purpose tempered a new consciousness that embraced the complexity and flux of life experience. Charles Darwin's theory of evolution, first published in 1859, affirmed the inevitability of process, of a continual state of becoming, but a Victorian faith in progress still promised a teleological unity. A number of historians have discussed how modernism, especially the American variety, posited a radical integration of those dichotomies which Victorians assumed severed forever: civilization and savagery, male and female, technology and nature, object and self, knowledge and intuition, aestheticism and spirituality, illusion and authenticity. Although American modernism acknowledged the chaos of modern life, it did not apocalyptically succumb to its irrationality. Instead, *fin-de-siècle* modernists offered, through the subjective lens of artistic sensibility, a therapeutic vision that abated the disjunction and dissolution prophesied by Marx.[18]

An overview of the four essays included in this volume will suggest how America's supreme cultural event of 1893 and her artists conjoined in a reluctant modernist response to the concerns of the era.

In "The American Personality in the Age of American Impressionism" Sarah Burns rightly notes how the popularity of the modern painted portrait corresponded to the new age of consumerism. Outward appearances, behavior, and typecasting became supremely important during a period in which established social hierarchies seemed threatened by immigrant influx, labor disputes, and technological innovations. Such society portraitists as Cecilia Beaux, William Merritt Chase, and John Singer Sargent accommodated the period's desire for a "unique" personality that could be instantly recognized as "American" *and* the highest civilized ideal. Their seemingly personal recording of immediate sensations and feelings through the painterly brush betokened an authenticity that was increasingly absent in an age of mechanical reproduction and corporate bureaucracy. To contemporary observers their portraits' animated surfaces signified the nervous energy and restless pace of the American, just as clothing, gesture, and physiognomy communicated gender, breeding, and race. Yet all elements were codes to create a product to be consumed rather than reveal any truth within. The critic who regarded Chase's virtuoso surfaces as evidence of a talent at once "superficial" and "brilliant" and therefore essentially "of artistic 'modernity' as of modern life" unwittingly proclaimed the importance of spectacle to *fin-de-siècle* American modernism. Like the World's Columbian Exposition, society portraiture in the age of Impressionism marketed surface display, indomitable energy, cultural refinement, material abundance, and Anglo-Saxon superiority as the modern American spectacle.

Such promotion of social and racial types took on a loudly popular tone at the Chicago fair. Just as the fair's impermanent buildings made of staff offered

European architectural styles for public consumption, so too did its varied exhibitions present cultural types from all over the world for the predominantly white, middle-class crowd to survey. Photographic portfolios commemorating the fair, such as J. W. Buel's *The Magic City*, mimic the catalogue-like display of peoples offered by the village exhibitions and performances of the Midway Plaisance. Emulating arranged postcards or a strip of penny photos, each page presents an array of racial and cultural models. Moor, Egyptian, Bulgarian, Turk, Norwegian, and Japanese pose side by side, yet each is contained within its own divided border; their costumes, facial features, and postures (the Persians invariably recline) impress their respective racial and cultural characters. Rarely do text or image, however, distinguish the individual from the type. Labeled "picturesque types" or "other types of the midway," as well as "characters in the midway," "types of all nations," and "a procession of the nations," souvenir photographic surveys of "nearly every semi-civilized type of the world" imitate the consumerist display of modern, industrial goods assembled in the Court of Honor's buildings (Fig. 5). They create a tension between the assemblage of ethnic individuals and the visual rhetoric of Western culture; poses tend to replicate the conventions of European portraiture; and backdrops are usually a classical porch or ornate Baroque furniture. Marketing codes rather than truths for consumption, these photographic albums operate on the same assumptions as *fin-de-siècle* society portraiture. Like the Midway spectacle they mirrored, the fair's souvenir albums objectify the unique, transforming it into the category of "the other." They permitted the fairgoer and those who missed seeing the real thing to accomplish what the heroine of Burnham's *Sweet Clover* could only voice as she viewed a performance at the Chinese Theater: "I want one of those brown girls to take home as bricabrac."[19]

How easily the individual could be converted into a type of ornament was evident in the Midway's display of "varied types of beauty" at the International Dress and Costume Company's exhibition (Fig. 6). In such an exhibition, as a photograph from the fair attests, the attribution of beauty and race depended primarily upon the surface display of costume and pose. Unlike the "types of all nations" in the souvenir albums, physiognomy plays a minimal role in distinguishing the figures. In fact, the Oriental type here has neither the Middle Eastern nor the Far Eastern facial features and skin coloring that would truly separate her from her European companions. Instead, the Oriental's center stage-like position, active stance, and tamborine identify her as the exotic type who performed dances at the midway side shows. The Englishwoman represents an Anglo-Saxon counterpart. Her averted gaze, demure stance, clasped hands, and floral adornments identify her as a model of elegant femininity and deportment. Her turned head, trailing skirt, and asymmetrical placement sug-

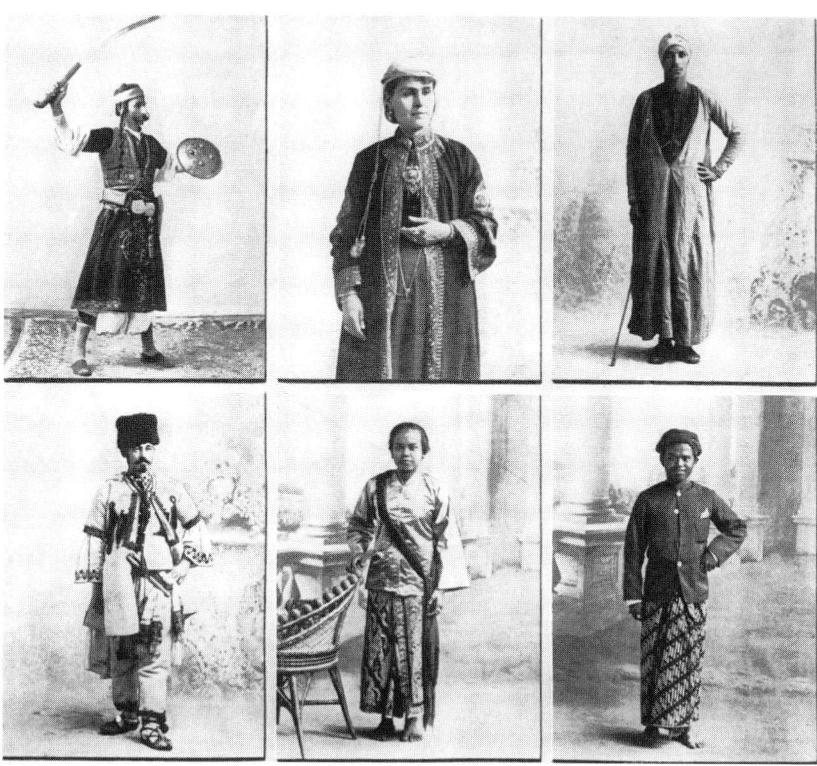

FIGURE 5 *Picturesque Types of the Midway*, photograph from *The Magic City*, J.W. Buel. Historical Publishing Company, 1894.

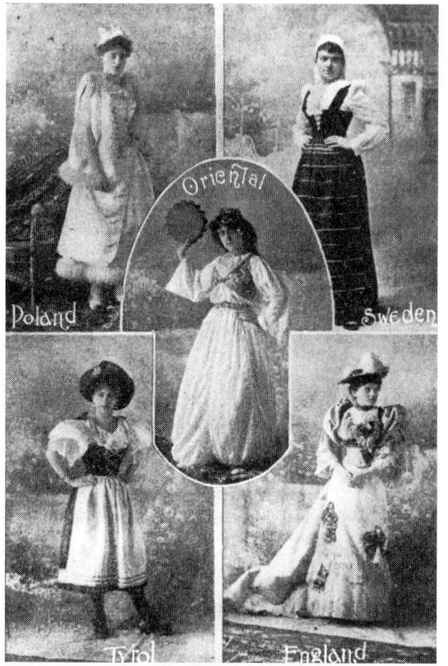

FIGURE 6 *Types of Beauty*, photograph from *The World's Columbian Exposition, Chicago, 1893*, Trumball White, *et al.* American Publishing House, 1893.

gest that she may glide out of the frame at any moment (and that she desperately wishes to do so). She obviously does not belong with the other(s).

The emergence of a modern American type amended the tradition of Anglo-Saxon femininity paraded at the costume display. The New Woman, as she was called, assumed a directness of manner and freedom of dress that expressed her new social ambitions. She appeared in such diverse forms as Charles Gibson's magazine illustrations of the "Gibson Girl," John Singer Sargent's society portrait of Mrs. Isaac Phelps Stokes, and Mary Cassatt's mural of modern woman for the World's Columbian Exposition. Yet an ambivalent and conservative reaction to the changing status of women in American society is evident even in those who were associated with exalting her modern position. As Nancy Matthews argues in "Mary Cassatt and the Changing Face of the 'Modern Woman' in the Impressionist Era," Cassatt, regarded by her contemporaries as the quintessential modern woman artist, tempered her own depictions of the new woman during the *fin de siècle*. Her earlier images of women in independent acts of self-absorbed reading disappear in favor of images of community and domesticity. Although Cassatt was always pro-suffrage and supported aspiring women artists, she defined the modern woman in a manner antithetical to the physically and morally liberated women who rode bicycles and smoked cigarettes. Genteel deportment and feminine culture restrained the radical potential of the modern woman. In Cassatt's turn-of-the-century images and in that representation of the American "woman's declaration of independence," the Woman's Building of the Chicago world's fair, women were defined as the overseers of civilization.[20]

The Woman's Building was supposed to place the modern American woman on a level of accomplishment equal to the modern male's. The fact that its Italian Renaissance design was created by Sophia Hayden, the first woman to graduate from the Massachusetts Institute of Technology's program in architectural design, and that all of its decorations were executed by women, would seem to suggest that it was successful. Its placement, however, as the gateway between the Midway and the "White City," signified woman as the mediator between the savage, exotic, and carnival-like world of "the other" and the refined, domesticated, and cultured world of Western civilization.[21] The building itself communicated an ideal type of womanhood that was far from embracing the complex identities, social freedoms, and professional ambitions of the emerging modern woman (or modern man). Candace Wheeler, patron of the decorative arts movement, observed how the Woman's Building was "the most peacefully human of all the buildings. . .like a man's ideal of woman—delicate, dignified, pure, and fair to look upon."[22] Its sculptural decoration reinforced her claim:

pediment figures sculpted in high relief represented such "Woman's Virtues" as sacrifice, charity, maternity, and love, as well as "Woman as the Spirit of Civilization."[23]

Inside, a series of mural paintings continued the theme of woman as civilizer, especially Mary Cassatt's *Modern Woman* (Fig. 7) which was consciously paired with Mary Fairchild MacMonnies's *Primitive Woman*, directly across the main hall (Fig. 8). MacMonnies's half-naked women clad in classical drapery carried waterjugs, plowed and sowed the fields, and attended to the thirst of a male hunter who just returned with game. MacMonnies explained the significance of such movements: "The women indicate with the completest possible simplicity the bearer of burdens, the toilers of the earth, the servants of man, and more than this, being without ambition, contented with their lot." Although imbued with classical form and grace, the figures recalled in their activities the tribal communities on display in the Midway. Indeed, MacMonnies's admission that she rejected "the idea of the savage, the prehistoric, the slave, the Oriental woman," and avoided detailing any one "race or environment," placing her figures "in a landscape background that might be of any time or country and is certainly not in America,"[24] suggests that the abstract idea she wished to convey was allied to that of the Midway: there exists a multitude of lowly, uncivilized cultures that have yet to (and will probably never on their own) match the progressive achievements of Chicago's "White City."

Cassatt's three-panel composition of women and young girls in contemporary dress, however, used the motifs of harvesting, barefoot play, and artistic performance to suggest a community of cultural and intellectual nurturance not unlike that found in the women's colleges of the day. *Young Women Plucking the Fruits of Knowledge and Science* flanked by *Young Girls Pursuing Fame* and *The Arts, Music, and Dancing* implied that the New Woman, through education in an exclusively female community, could rise above her traditional sphere as domestic caretaker. Yet her new responsibility would be to effect the progress of the entire family of man. Without her efforts the "savage" tribes of the Midway could never rise to the high achievement of the civilized Court of Honor, overseen by yet another image of woman, the sixty-five foot gilded statue representing the republic by Daniel Chester French.[25] Cassatt's mural received much criticism for its garish colors, Japanese effect, obscure subject, and depiction of women independent from the society of men. It marked Cassatt as the lowest manifestation of the New Woman type. She assaulted the eye with "impudent greens and brutal blues," suggestive of "an aggressive personality with which compromise and cooperation would be impossible."[26] On the other hand, MacMonnies presented an integrated, soothing decoration that communicated an

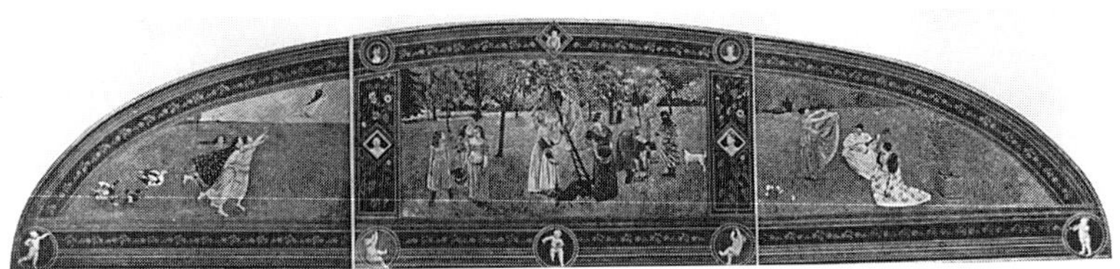

FIGURE 7 Mary Cassatt, *Modern Woman*, halftone from *Art and Handicraft at the Woman's Building of the World's Columbian Exposition, 1893,* Maud Howe Elliot, ed. Chicago Historical Society.

appropriate reverance towards womanhood. Still, Cassatt belied traditional Victorian notions of femininity when she defended her images to Mrs. Bertha Palmer: "Men I have no doubt are painted in all their vigor on the walls of other buildings; to us the sweetness of childhood, the charm of womanhood [are important], if I have not conveyed some sense of that charm, in one word if I have not been absolutely feminine, then I have failed."[27]

As if to evoke the future generations of modern women and assert an essential femininity, Cassatt decorated the border of her allegory with Italianate medallions featuring portraits of women and young babies in various poses of play. Only that section of her work received the positive commentary of being "charming" and "beautifully painted." It is not surprising, therefore, that Cassatt found her greatest success after the turn of the century with images of attractive mothers and appealing children as Matthews indicates, creating a readily digested image of the feminine that provided an antidote to societal fears about the New Woman. In effect, Cassatt's artistic modernity became increasingly subdued as it succumbed to the restraining impulses of common social types.

Exotic landscapes and cultures could be made familiar and less threatening if they too were subsumed into the order of a greater whole and made comprehensible as a type. At the Chicago World's Columbian Exposition, the Midway Plaisance offered the exotica of various societies as entertainment, easily consumed and non-threatening to the fair's essential assertion of a Western European, ethnographic superiority. America's own diversity of landscapes and cultural regions found expression in the fair's many state buildings, exhibitions, and congresses. Yet such variety was not permitted to overshadow the message of the "White City:" the promise of a cohesive, modern American empire.

Of the many significant meetings at the World's Columbian Exposition of 1893, that of the American Historical Association was the most notable. At that gathering Frederick Jackson Turner presented his influential "frontier thesis," in which he declared the West and its mastery single-handedly responsible for the formation of the inventive, energetic, individualistic American self. By 1893 the

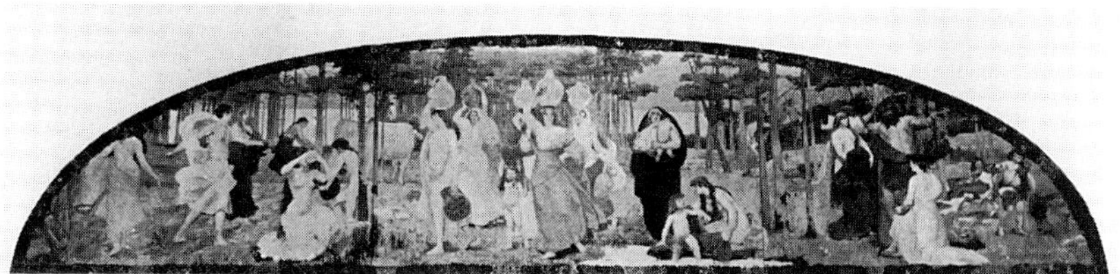

FIGURE 8 Mary MacMonnies, *Primitive Woman*, photograph from *Art and Handicraft
in the Woman's Building of the World's Columbian Exposition, 1893,*
Maud Howe Elliot, ed. Chicago Historical Society.

West had been won from its "savage" inhabitants and made subject to those
forces of progress represented in the "White City" of the fair and the "Black
City" of Chicago. In the same year Thomas Moran reinterpreted the Grand
Canyon of the Yellowstone in an aesthetic mode that owed much to Impression-
ism; by doing so, he began a trend that, as Charles Eldredge points out in
"American Impressionism Goes West," would reinvigorate both the "closed"
Western frontier and Impressionist style.

True to Turner's "frontier thesis," American Impressionism participated in an
aesthetic westward expansion. Thanks to the experiments of such New England
painters as Childe Hassam and John Twachtman, it culminated in the triumph
of Impressionism at San Francisco's Panama-Pacific International Exposition of
1915 and in the West's burgeoning art colonies. As Eldredge demonstrates,
Hassam, Twachtman, and others renewed their individual Impressionist modes
by turning their eyes to Oregon's Harney Desert, the hot pools of Yellowstone
National Park, and the California coast. In their inventive application of a style
originally formed on French soil to a harsher American environment, these
westward-turning Impressionists displayed those traits that Turner associated
with the American's essential frontier identity born from subduing a wilderness
and converting it into an urban society:

> ...coarseness and strength combined with acuteness and inquisitiveness, that prac-
> tical, inventive turn of mind, quick to find expedients, that masterful grasp of ma-
> terial things, lacking in the artistic but powerful to effect great ends, that restless,
> nervous energy, that dominant individualism...that buoyancy and exuberance
> which comes from freedom....[28]

Indeed, fresh from his visit to the World's Columbian Exposition, the influential critic and novelist Hamlin Garland attributed similar traits to the American Impressionist in his *Crumbling Idols, Twelve Essays on Art* of 1894. Born and
raised in the West, Garland employed a rhetoric that turned the American Impressionist into a rugged individualist who, with "vivid and fearless coloring"

and "an advance in the perceptive power of the human eye," transformed nature into a new world. He declared the Impressionist "an iconoclast" who "deals with the present:"

> He has no conventional pictures, full of impossible juxtapositions. He takes fresh, vital themes, mainly out-of-door scenes. He aims always at freshness and vigor. The impressionist is a buoyant and cheerful painter. He loves the open air, and the mid-day sun. He has little to say about the "mystery" and "sentiment" of nature. His landscapes quiver with virile color. He emphasizes (too often over-emphasizes) his difference in method by choosing the most gorgeous subjects. At his worst, the impressionist is daring in his choice of subject and over-assertive in his handling.[29]

To many observers the master organizers of the Chicago World's Columbian Exposition exhibited a comparable boldness in their erection of the dazzling "White City" on a Chicago swamp. In language evoking Turner's theory of frontier expansion, John Ingalls summarized in "Lessons of the Fair" a pervasive sentiment of incredulous wonder at "the wealth, courage and audacious energy of Chicago," its "undaunted spirit" that "proved equal to every emergency" as it created a "gorgeous arena" from "the worthless suburb of a squalid hamlet upon the far frontier." "The conception was Napoleonic, and the result is an epoch in history." It was a triumph "for the new empire of the West, of which Chicago is the foreordained metropolis."[30] In the "White City" Chicago's barren plains and harsh stockyards were transfigured into an ideal spectacle of light, order, and refinement. The familiarity of classical architectural language made strikingly America's own in its multiplicity of associations, and the coherence afforded by white staff, turned the difficulties of the modern city into a dream vision more palatable than any reality. So, too, the American Impressionists who went West applied to an exotic and severe landscape a style that had grown in popularity and acceptance, and that was adapted from European roots to individual temperament. By doing so, they ironically endowed a unity and familiarity to the frontier. The West became modern yet domesticated; it became a stylistic type—an Impressionist landscape.

A similar transformation took place as Impressionism was applied to the modern urban environment. As Kathleen Pyne argues in "Social Conflict and American Painting in the Age of Darwin," American Impressionists offered a secure, civilized, and restorative world to those citizens shaken by the cacophony of American social and economic change. Twachtman, Weir, Hassam, and Chase expunged from their art the violence ascribed to French Impressionism and the chaos associated with the modern city populated by immigrants. The therapeutic and filiopietistic character of their art extended that desire for repose and harmony American cultural critics first loudly voiced in the New York art periodical, *The Crayon* (1855-1861), during an earlier period of dramatic national development.[31] In accommodating the Victorian need for repose and order, the American Impressionists created a new type of urban landscape—an organic one that synthesized city and country.[32] It is not surprising, then, that the restrained modernity of the World's Columbian Exposition inspired Twachtman, Weir, Hassam, and Chase to render its grand monuments, green spaces, and quiet waters; significantly, they avoided the raucous, crowded Midway.

As we have seen, the Chicago world's fair of 1893 represented for many an ideal to which the modern city could aspire. Neil Harris has noted how "the fair was a city that worked."[33] It permitted a transcendence of dirt, disorder, poverty, and instability. It could even redeem that "sink-hole of the sewage of humanity," as Charles Kurtz, key organizer of the fair's art exhibition, characterized Chicago and its residents.[34] The fair presented itself as an object lesson for emulation, an ideal type comparable to the other social and landscape types of *fin-de-siècle* American culture. William Dean Howells perceived the Chicago fair in just this way. It seemed purposely designed as an emblem of beauty and civility. Simply operated, perfectly policed, and thoroughly clean, it was "so little American in the accepted sense."[35] Neither the "White City's" classical grace nor the Midway's "primitive" types, Impressionism's fashionable personalities nor urban scenes expressed that "panting energy and inexhaustible impulse" that Bourget and others regarded as endemic to the modern American city.[36] The Chicago fair, like the entrepreneurial models of society portraiture, kept America's restless, diverse energies in check.

In "A New World Fable," fellow *Cosmopolitan* writer Hjalmar Boysen more fully captured the mythic nature of the fair. The "White City" was not only an ideal type but also a grand spectacle. When lit up at night by the miracle of electrical power, "it is a radiant vision of beauty, which fills the soul and which one is the better for having seen." The contentment of such a vision provided hope that America would with certainty and composure rise above its modest rural origins and enter the modern age of the century to come.[37] For, as another writer of 1893 recognized, electricity was "the symbol and stamp" of the American type, making him "a new man not a new Englishman;" he possessed the power to "electrify more races of men than any other." But all of his nervous energy made the American, "more than any other people to-day. . . .hungry for rest."[38] The World's Columbian Exposition, like American painting at the turn of the century, demonstrated that such contradictory aspects could be accommodated at once. The electric-powered Ferris wheel and commercial babel of the Midway Plaisance embodied modernity's consumptive energies. The light-reflecting lagoons and cool, classical facades of the "White City" supplied a timeless tranquility. In short, the World's Columbian Exposition, like the American Impressionists' urban renditions, asserted that America could embrace modernity without the disruption Marx pronounced as its necessary attendant.

The promise that Bourget and others saw in the "White City" and American Impressionism was to be effaced as the present became the past, as the nineteenth century gave way to the twentieth. Twenty years after the World's Columbian Exposition and two years before American Impressionism's coronation as a national style at the Panama-Pacific International Exposition, another cultural event shook American expectations of what the modern age would bring. *The International Exhibition of Modern Art*, organized by the Association of American Painters and Sculptors, opened in New York City on February 17, 1913, at the 69th Regiment Armory. It prompted Mabel Dodge to announce to Gertrude Stein: "There is an exhibition coming off which is the most important public event that has ever come off since the signing of the Declaration of Independence, and it is of the same nature. . . .There will be a riot and a revolution and things will never be quite the same afterwards."[39] Both radicals and conservatives associated the Armory Show with anarchic revolt. This massive exhibition of sixteen hundred works of modern art from Eugène Delacroix to Marcel Duchamp aroused fear rather than wonder about the future of culture and civilization in America. Few viewers were prepared for the radical revision of form and space to be seen in the cubist room, dubbed the "chamber of horrors" by the press. American artists were threatened as well by the Europeans' enthusiastic seizure of the ambiguities of modernism. The Armory Show made clear that America had not out-Europed Europe but instead had remained locked into a Victorian, reluctant modernism that was unwilling to renounce established types. Regarding the American section of the exhibition, William Glackens despaired of America's hestitancy to break with decorum and to embrace the contingency of modernity: "Our own art is arid and bloodless. It is like nothing so much as dry bones. It shows that we are afraid to be impulsive, afraid to forget restraint, afraid above everything to appear ridiculous."[40]

If one of the most controversial images of the Chicago fair was Mary Cassatt's mural of *Modern Woman* because it reimagined the role of women in society with a visual language deemed too strident, it was no match for the modernity of Marcel Duchamp's *Nude Descending a Staircase, No. 2* (Fig. 9), the most talked-about work of art in the Armory Show. Duchamp's *Nude* shattered form and space, confounded the organic and the mechanical, and therby perplexed and frightened the spectator. Moreover, it radically questioned the nature of

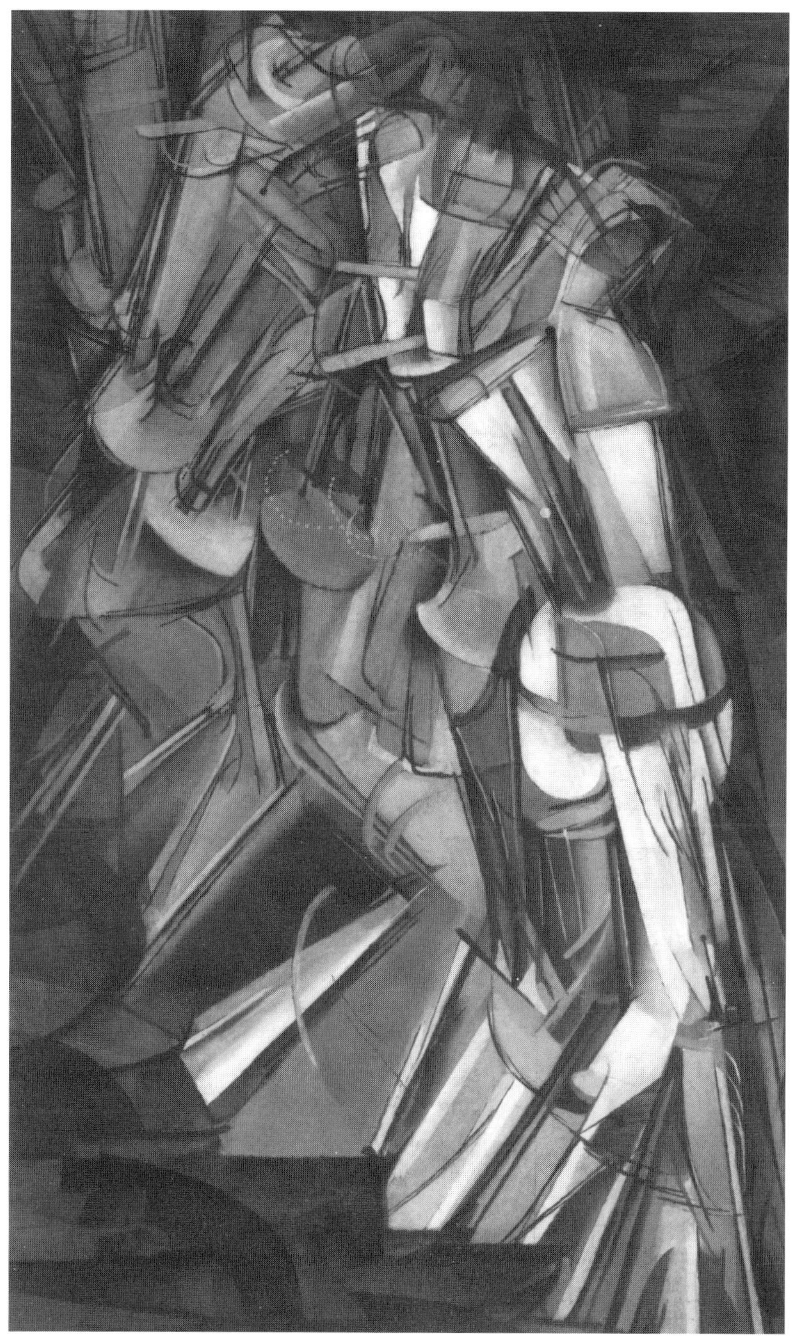

FIGURE 9 Marcel Duchamp, *Nude Descending a Staircase*, 1912. Oil on canvas. Philadelphia Museum of Art, Collection of Louise and Walter Arensberg.

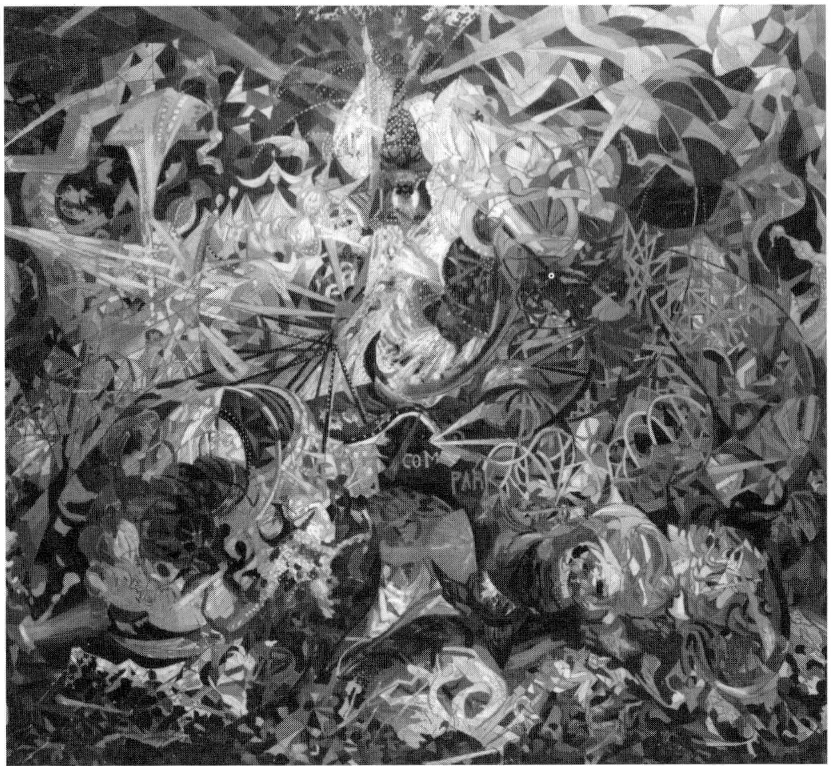

FIGURE 10 Joseph Stella, *Battle of Lights, Coney Island, Mardi Gras*, 1913-14.
Oil on canvas. Yale University Art Gallery, bequest of Dorothea Dreier to the
Collection Société Anonyme.

gender itself. Of the many attempts at deciphering Duchamp's painting, it was
the poem submitted to *The American Art News* which detected Duchamp's an-
drogynous redefinition of the traditional nude:

> You've tried to find her
> And you've looked in vain
> Up the picture and down again,
> You've tried to fashion her of broken bits,
> And you've worked yourself into seventeen fits;
> The reason you've failed to tell you I can,
> It isn't a lady but only a man.[41]

Mary Cassatt refashioned the image of woman by drawing upon the established notions of female nurturer and cultural purveyor. Duchamp abandoned

traditional categories altogether. For many Americans, Duchamp's *Nude Descending a Staircase* exemplified that confusion of identity endemic to the modern age.

Unlike the World's Columbian Exposition, the Armory Show presented images that radically broke with established types. In fact, the individual reigned rather than the type; so too did questions rather than solutions, uncertainities rather than promises, the ridiculous rather than the ideal. In 1913, Joseph Stella's cacophonous *Battle of Lights, Coney Island* (Fig. 10) superseded Twachtman's dreamy *Court of Honor* as cultural emblem. The technology responsible for the Chicago fair's wondrous electric light displays was now directed to producing the mass destruction of the war machine. The promised utopia of 1893 had crumpled under the fierce, chaotic realities of the modern age.

This essay is dedicated to the memory of Steve Simon (1915-1993), a father who always kept his promises.

NOTES

1   Paul Bourget, "A Farewell to the White City," *The Cosmopolitan* 16 (December 1893): 133, 135-37, 140. I would like to thank William U. Eiland, Donald Keyes, and especially Sarah Burns for their helpful editorial suggestions.

2   There are a number of important interpretive histories of the World's Columbian Exposition. This essay is indebted to the work of those scholars, especially David F. Burg, Neil Harris, Robert W. Rydell, and the late David C. Huntington, whose unpublished lectures continue to be an inspiration. On the unique characteristics of American Impressionism, see H. Barbara Weinberg, Doreen Bolger, and David Park Curry, *American Impressionism and Realism: The Painting of Modern Life*, 1885-1915 (New York: The Metropolitan Museum of Art & Harry N. Abrams, 1994), 8-9, 14-19.

3   Numerous paintings by Theodore Robinson, Childe Hassam, and Willard Metcalf capture the typical American Impressionist's view of the World's Columbian Exposition with its ever-moving crowds, brilliant light reflections, and expansive park spaces.

4   Burg points out how the press made explicit references to the World's Columbian Exposition as a realization of the Heavenly City, and in effect, the New Jerusalem. See David F. Burg, *Chicago's White City of 1893* (Lexington: University Press of Kentucky, 1976), 113.

5   Robert W. Rydell, "Rediscovering the 1893 Chicago World's Columbian Exposition," in *Revisiting the White City* (Washington, D.C.: Smithsonian Institution, 1993), 49.

6   W[illiam] D[ean] Howells, "Letters of an Alturian Traveller, II," *The Cosmopolitan* 16 (December 1893): 222.

7 Julian Ralph, *Harper's Chicago and the World's Fair* (New York: Harper and Brothers, 1893) quoted in Curtis M. Hinsley, "The World as Marketplace: Commodification of the Exotic at the World's Columbian Exposition, Chicago, 1893," in *Exhibiting Cultures: The Poetics and Politics of Museum Display*, ed. Ivan Karp and Steven D. Lavine (Washington, D.C.: Smithsonian Institution Press, 1991), 351. For an extended discussion of this passage, see 351-53.

8 Clara Louisa Burnham, *Sweet Clover* (Chicago: Laird and Lee, 1893), 201, quoted in Rydell, *Revisiting the White City*, 55.

9 Quoted in Hinsley, "The World as Marketplace," 346.

10 The description is that of painter Will H. Low, "The Art of the White City," *Scribner's Magazine*, 14 (July-December 1893): 512.

11 Quoted in Peter Conn, *The Divided Mind: Ideology and Imagination in America, 1898-1917* (Cambridge: Cambridge University Press, 1983), 9.

12 Bourget, "A Farewell to the White City," 140; Howells voiced similar hopes but was more skeptical of America's ability to cultivate a beauty which would transcend her essentially commercial and competitive nature. See Howells, "Letters of an Alturian Traveller, II," 221-222, 230.

13 E. C. Stedman, *The Critic* 23 (November 25, 1893): 333, quoted in Elizabeth Broun and Alan Fern, "Introduction," *Revisiting the White City*, 13.

14 For a comprehensive discussion of the exhibition, especially its organizational planning and jury composition, see Carolyn Kinder Carr, "Prejudice and Pride: Presenting American Art at the 1893 Chicago World's Columbian Exposition," in *Revisiting the White City*, 63-123.

15 Carr, "Prejudice and Pride," 78, 100.

16 Tonalism is a mode of painting during the *fin de siècle* distinguished for its emphasis on a quietistic mood, subtle gradations of color, poetic repose, and an "envelope" of atmosphere. Many of the artists now properly given this designation were at the time associated with American Impressionism: John Twachtman, Thomas Dewing, Dwight Tryon, George Inness, and James McNeill Whistler, among others. See Wanda M. Corn, *The Color of Mood: American Tonalism 1880-1910* (San Francisco: M. H. De Young Memorial Museum and the California Palace of the Legion of Honor, 1972).

17 Quoted in Marshall Berman, *All That Is Solid Melts Into Air: The Experience of Modernity* (New York: Simon and Shuster, 1982), 21.

18 The term "reluctant modernism" is from George Cotkin, *Reluctant Modernism: American Thought and Culture, 1880-1900.* (New York: Twayne Publishers, 1992), xi-xiv, *passim.* On the role of Darwinism, see 1-20 and 35-40. On American modernism, see also Malcolm Bradbury, "Struggling Westward: America and the Coming of Modernism" (I & II), *Encounter* 60 (January & February 1983): 55-60; 57-65; Daniel J. Singal, "Towards a Definition of American Modernism," *American Quarterly* 39 (Spring 1987): 5-26. Recently, Ann Douglas has asserted that America "had been modern long before modernism existed anywhere else" but hid it behind a veneer of Victorianism. After World War I America fully revealed a robust modernism. See Ann

Douglas, *Terrible Honesty: Mongrel Manhattan in the 1920s* (New York: Farrar, Straus & Giroux, 1995).

19 Burnham, *Sweet Clover*, 305, as quoted in Judy Sund, "Columbus and Columbia in Chicago, 1893: Man of Genius Meets Generic Woman," *The Art Bulletin* 75 (September 1993): 456, f.n. 87. In this article Sund contributes a number of significant insights to the issue of the fair's conflicting images of gender and societal roles, see 443-466.

20 Thomas Palmer, President of the National Commission for the World's Columbian Exposition and a long supporter of pro-suffragette interests, put the Woman's Building in such a context. See Jeanne Madeline Weimann, *The Fair Women* (Chicago: Academy Chicago, 1981), 278.

21 Robert W. Rydell, "A Cultural Frankenstein? The Chicago World's Columbian Exposition of 1893," in *Grand Illusions: Chicago's World's Fair of 1893* (Chicago: Chicago Historical Society, 1993), 156-157; see 151-157 for a further discussion of the social and racial implications of the Woman's Building; Alan Trachtenberg, *The Incorporation of America: Culture and Society in the Gilded Age* (New York: Hill and Wang, 1982), 221-222.

22 Quoted in Trachtenberg, *Incorporation of America*, 221.

23 Trumbull White and William Igleheart, *The World's Columbian Exposition, Chicago, 1893* (Philadelphia: American Publishing House, 1893), 447.

24 Quoted in Weimann, *The Fair Women*, 206-207.

25 This discourse of contemporary American women as necessary civilizers was further supported in the four decorative panels by American artists Lucia Fairchild, Amanda Brewster Sewell, Rosina Emmet Sherwood, and Lydia Emmet located on the sides of the hall: *The Women of Plymouth* spun flax, washed buckets, and taught their young girls together; *Arcadia* had classical figures carry water, pick fruit, and relax among goats; *The Republic's Welcome to Her Daughters* had a classically-garbed woman bestowing laurels upon contemporary women of accomplishment whether as artists or mothers; *Art, Science, and Literature* depicted a group of modern women actually engaged in creative activities. For contemporary illustrations and commentary, see Maud Howe Elliott, ed. *Art and Handicraft in the Woman's Building of the World's Columbian Exposition* (Paris & New York: Boussod, Valadon & Co., 1893), 24-33.

26 Henry B. Fuller, *Chicago Record*, quoted in Weimann, *The Fair Women*, 316. For an overview of the marked contrast in response to the two murals, see 314-319. See also Sund, "Columbus and Columbia in Chicago," 457-465.

27 Mary Cassatt to Bertha Plamer, September 10, 1892, quoted in Weimann, *The Fair Women*, 200.

28 Frederick Jackson Turner, "The Significance of the Frontier in American History," delivered at the meeting of the American Historical Association in Chicago, July 12, 1893, in *History, Frontier, and Section: Three Essays by Frederick Jackson Turner*, intro. Martin Ridge (Albuquerque: University of New Mexico Press, 1993), 87-88.

29 Hamlin Garland, *Crumbling Idols, Twelve Essays on Art Dealing Chiefly with Literature, Painting and the Drama*, ed. by Jane Johnson (1894; Cambridge, Mass.: Belknap

Press of Harvard University Press, 1960), 109, 104, 105.

30 John J. Ingalls, "Lessons of the Fair," *The Cosmopolitan* 16 (December 1893): 142-43.

31 On *The Crayon*'s call for a revitalized, idealized landscape full of light, breadth, and repose, see Janice Simon, "*The Crayon* 1855-1861: The Voice of Nature in Criticism, Poetry, and the Fine Arts" (Ph. D. dissertation, University of Michigan, 1990).

32 On America's repression of the city, see also Hubert Beck, "Urban Iconongraphy in Nineteenth-Century American Painting," in *American Icons: Transatlantic Perspectives on Eighteenth- and Nineteenth-Century American Art*, ed. Thomas W. Gaehtgens and Heinz Ickstadt (Santa Monica: Getty Center for the History of Art and the Humanities, 1992), 319-47.

33 Neil Harris, *Cultural Excursions: Marketing Appetites and Cultural Tastes in Modern America* (Chicago and London: The University of Chicago Press, 1990), 119.

34 Quoted in Carr, "Prejudice and Pride," 73.

35 Howells, "Letters of an Alturian Traveller, II," 221-22.

36 Bourget, "A Farewell to the White City," 136. It would take another decade for an artist like George Bellows to appear and transcend the inhibitions of reluctant modernism and its portrayal of marketable American types. His violent boxing pictures and tenement scenes of sloppy, crude immigrants provided an antipode to the polite world of the Chicago fair, its souvenir albums, and American Impressionism.

37 Hjalmar Boysen, "A New World Fable," *The Cosmopolitan* 16 (December 1893): 179, 186.

38 H. G. Cutler, "The American Not a New Englishman, But a New Man," *New England Magazine*, new series 9 (September 1893): 29-31.

39 Mabel Dodge to Gertrude Stein, January 24, 1913, quoted in Martin Green, *New York 1913* (New York: Collier Books, Macmillan, 1988), 95.

40 William J. Glackens, "The American Section," *Arts and Decoration* (March 1913): 159 in *The Armory Show; International Exhibition of Modern Art, 1913*, vol. 3, *Contemporary & Retrospective Documents* (New York: Arno Press, 1972), n.p.

41 Quoted in Milton W. Brown, *The Story of the Armory Show* (New York: Joseph H. Hirshorn Foundation, 1963), 110. The poem won ten dollars for its inventive explanation of Duchamp's painting.

Mary Cassatt and the Changing Face of
The "Modern Woman" in the Impressionist Era

NANCY MATHEWS

———

BORN IN 1844, Mary Cassatt was of a generation that doggedly defined itself as "modern" even when, in its old age in the first decades of the twentieth century, there were other, younger generations clamoring to take the title away. In her youth she behaved with a reckless freedom that her elders accepted as characteristic of a new era. When she was middle-aged, she pictured the "modern woman" as staid and responsible—just as she had become. When she was old, she campaigned for non-juried art exhibitions and women's suffrage, and disparaged all those who proposed a different definition of "modern art" or "modern woman" in the new century. In each of these three periods of her life, she used her art to reflect her notions of modernity, all the while balancing her own deeply held beliefs with the ever-changing art and ideas around her.

For the young Mary Cassatt the "face" of the modern woman was emphatically unimportant. When Edouard Manet and Edgar Degas portrayed Berthe Morisot and Cassatt in such works as *Berthe Morisot with a Fan*, 1872 (Musée d'Orsay) and *Mary Cassatt at the Louvre*, 1879 (Fig. 1), Morisot's face was obscured by the fan and Cassatt's back was to the viewer. While these were extreme cases, it was common in Impressionist paintings such as Cassatt's *Lydia Reading the Morning Paper*, 1878 (Joslyn Art Museum) and Morisot's *Reading*, 1873 (The Cleveland Museum of Art) for the face to be turned away or deliberately vague. Instead of routinely looking for the sitter's appeal in her face, the modern artist often found the defining characteristics of the modern woman in her pose, gesture, and activity. Often the pose was unladylike; the woman hunched her shoulders or crossed her legs in attitudes that women were not supposed to display in public.[1]

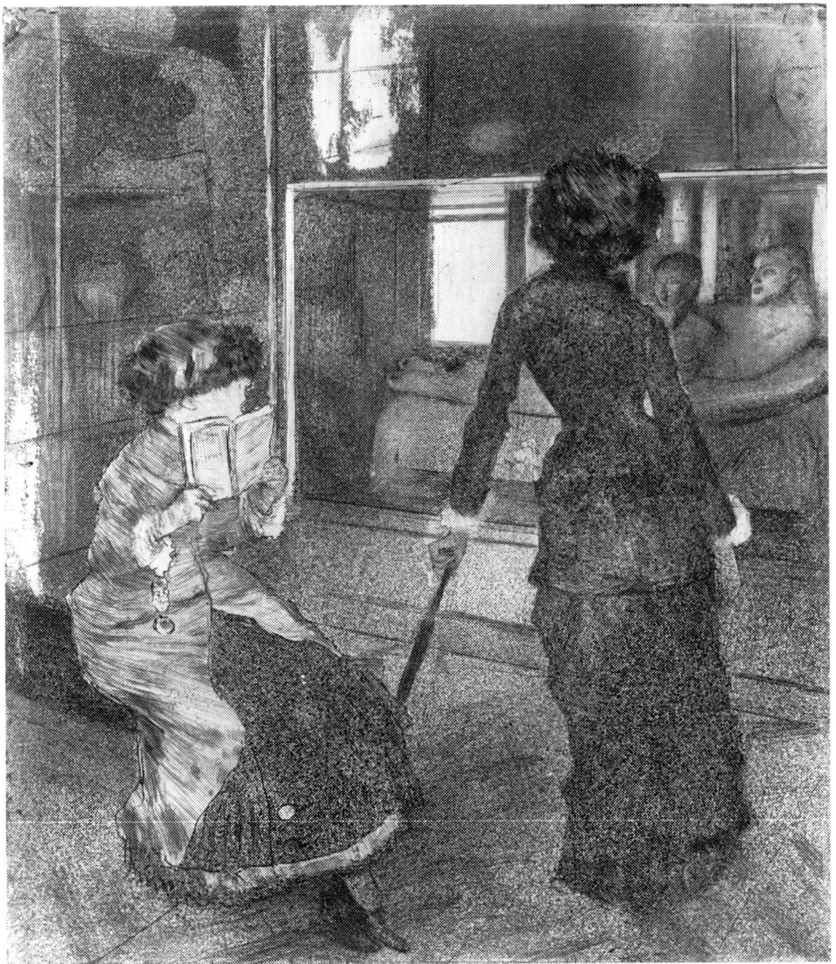

FIGURE 1 Edgar Degas, *At the Louvre: Mary Cassatt in the Etruscan Gallery*, 1879, Aquatint. Museum of Fine Arts, Boston.

Cassatt and Morisot were highly energetic, both physically and mentally, but they did not see themselves as extraordinary. Rather, they saw themselves as examples of the modern young woman, so well-recognized that she was often described in popular novels of the day. One well-known fictional character of this type was Renée Mauperin, of the eponymous novel of 1864 by Edmond and Jules de Goncourt. Renée was full of physical and mental vitality. She swam and rode horseback with the boys, and when she played the piano, she swayed vigorously with the popular dance music. When she offended a prospective suitor and angered her mother (who had worked hard to arrange the match) with her free and easy speech, a male friend defended her:

> We have quite finished, have we not, and when I say we, I mean the majority of the French people, with the pretty little young ladies who used to talk like mechanical dolls. . . all that sort of thing's done with, old-fashioned, worn out. . . . We ask a girl now about her impressions and we expect her to say what she thinks naturally and originally. . . . If she should have any talent it is encouraged and cultivated. Instead of ordinary governesses she must have good masters, professors from the Conservatoire, or artists whose pictures have been hung. . . . Come, now, isn't that the way girls are being educated now in middle-class society?[2]

Berthe Morisot and her sisters were raised exactly in this manner. They grew up in suburban Paris where they were given music lessons by the prestigious music professor Camille Stamaty and art lessons by the eminent landscape painter Jean-Baptiste Corot. They mixed with the artistic and literary intelligentsia who regularly attended Mme. Morisot's "Tuesday evenings." Berthe let it be known that she was not in the market for a husband, and thus the young men of her social and intellectual class found her irresistible. She could easily have been the model for the Goncourts' Renée, although she preferred to see herself as taking after her highly educated grandmother, Marie Caroline Mayniel, a woman of "a boyish frankness, a very lucid, very keen intelligence [who] didn't ever hesitate to speak boldly . . ."[3]

On the American side of the Atlantic, Mary Cassatt was similarly encouraged by her parents. After a childhood spent partially in Europe, she was sent to the prestigious Pennsylvania Academy of the Fine Arts at age sixteen. She rode horseback with her brothers and thought nothing of traveling around Philadelphia and the surrounding counties by herself to visit friends and to paint. Her literary counterpart—the American literary equivalent to Renée Mauperin—was Jo March, the boyish heroine of Louisa May Alcott's *Little Women*, an overnight success when first published in 1868. Like Renée, Jo March was physically energetic and entirely unself-conscious in her movements. When engaged in writing or any other mental activity, she showed no concern for conventional appearance. Sprawled on an old sofa in the attic, she read or wrote with vigorous attention: "Quite absorbed in her work, Jo scribbled away till the last page was filled, when she signed her name with a flourish, and threw down her pen, exclaiming,—'There, I've done my best!'"[4]

Mary Cassatt was similarly exuberant in her artistic pursuits. When in Paris in the 1860s, she fearlessly charged around the city at all hours to sit in on modeling sessions, copy in the museums, or seek guidance from well-known professors. The parents of one of the friends she dragged along with her were alarmed at Cassatt's unconventional behavior and wrote to warn their daughter about the hazards of following her lead: "I hope you will not run any risk of being waylaid or insulted. I fear that you with Miss Cassatt may venture too far, do not rely on her judgement . . . and from the impulse of a moment you may rush with her into things that may injure you."[5] Cassatt and her friends were well aware of the accomplishments of women artists of the past and present and did not hesitate to stand up to male colleagues who tried to relegate them to the background. When an older male student at the Pennsylvania Academy tried to tell Cassatt's friend Eliza Haldeman that a particular exercise was too hard for her, she dismissed his chauvinistic criticism. As she wrote her father, "Mr. Wharton came up and said 'I might as well try to cross Mount Blanc [highest mountain in the Alps] as to draw that head, it was the one of the hardest ones in the Academy.' I had a mind to tell him that no less than three ladies had crossed it . . . ."[6]

In the 1860s and early 1870s the radical artists such as Manet, Morisot, Monet, and Degas found ways of portraying the mental absorption and physical freedom so characteristic of the modern woman. When Cassatt began to learn this style in the later 1870s, after she had been invited to join the French Impressionists, but before her first exhibition with them, the evolution in her painting reveals how completely she mastered Impressionist devices. When Cassatt first attempted a modern portrait of her mother in *Le Figaro* in early 1878 (Private Collection, Fig. 2), she showed the sitter in a light-filled domestic setting reading the folded pages of the newspaper through the lenses of her pince-nez. Her face is clearly defined, and she sits upright in a consciously correct position. Although Mrs. Cassatt's quest for current information was a modern attribute, the propriety of her pose gives her an old-fashioned air. Almost two years later, after mastering the modern style, Cassatt returned to the subject in an etching, *Reading the Newspaper (No. 2)*, 1879-80, where her mother is seen from behind her right shoulder. This time her profile is almost lost as she devotes her full attention to the white newspaper pages spread out before her. She slumps in her chair with her feet up. Cassatt, by playing down her face and giving her a less conventional pose, brings her mother into the realm of the modern woman. In the related drawing *Under the Lamp* (Collection of Dr. and Mrs. Jeb Stewart, Fig. 3), Cassatt shows two figures—her mother and sister—ignoring not only the viewer but each other. Reading, listening, and indulging in moments of reflection were common subjects for the women among the Impressionists including not only Cassatt and Morisot but also Eva Gonzales and Marie Bracquemond.

The female artist was often viewed in the mid-nineteenth century as the quintessential modern woman. As women pressed for equal rights in Europe

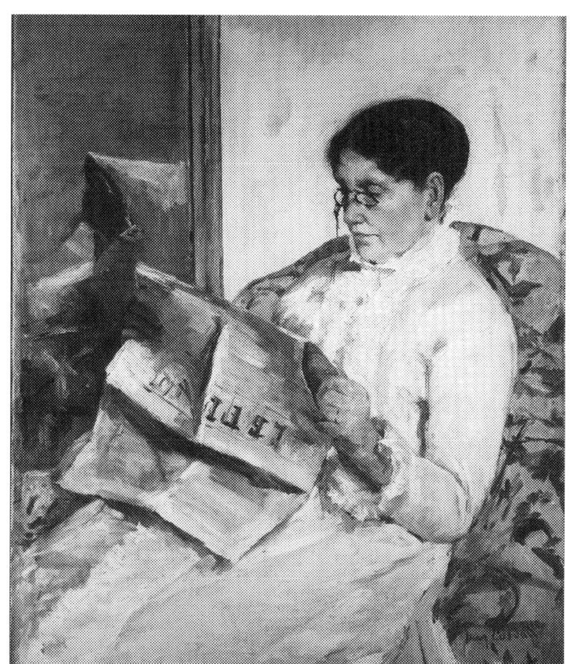

FIGURE 2 Mary Cassatt, *Reading Le Figaro*, 1877-78.
Oil on canvas. Private Collection, Washington, D.C.

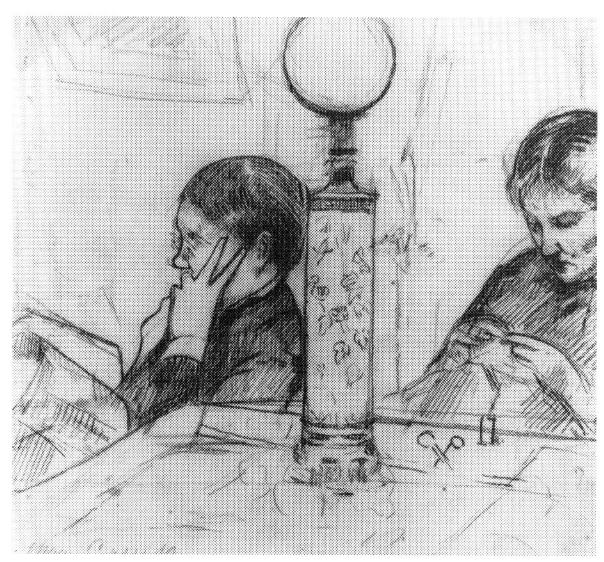

FIGURE 3 Mary Cassatt, *Under the Lamp (Two Women at the Lamp)*,
1880-82, Pencil on paper. Collection of Dr. and Mrs. Jeb Stewart.

and America in the 1840s and 1850s, they recognized the necessity for income-producing work for women of all classes. Lower-class women had long been swept up by the Industrial Revolution with factory work and urban employments such as running small retail shops, sewing, laundering, and domestic service. But middle and upper-class women who had received respectable educations had teaching as their only recourse if they could not or would not be supported by a man. By mid-century both writing and the visual arts were promoted as viable professions for these women.[7] Both offered a range of options, from commercial or industrial applications to the highly sought-after career as a fine artist. Anne Brönte's heroine in *The Tenant of Wildfell Hall*, 1848, parlays her artistic talent into the production of landscape paintings, which brought sufficient income to allow her to leave her abusive husband and strike out on her own. Nathaniel Hawthorne, in his 1860 classic, *The Marble Faun*, writes of two women artists in Rome who enjoyed the freedom women elsewhere desired. Hilda, a young American girl, moved about the city

> all alone, perfectly independent, under her own sole guardianship . . . doing what she liked, without a suspicion or a shadow upon the snowy whiteness of her fame. The customs of artist-life bestow such liberty upon the sex, which is elsewhere restricted within so much narrower limits; and it is perhaps an indication that, whenever we admit woman to a wider scope of pursuits and professions, we must also remove the shackles of our present conventional rules . . .[8]

The women artists in the French Impresssionist circle, having grown up with a sense of themselves as modern women, were fortunate to discover a style that conveyed their sense of physical and mental freedom from convention. But the style was also shaped by them. The men, whether painting the women artists or other women they knew well, were infected with the same spirit or style that all the women in their group brought with them. Manet, for instance, used his wife, Suzanne Leenhof, as an important model early in the development of his radical style. Monet went through a similar period of experimentation when painting his wife, Camille Doncieux. Leenhof was an independent woman when Manet met her; she was a pianist and piano teacher, and was bold enough to pose nude for her husband in an important early picture, *The Surprised Nymph* (Buenos Aires, M.N.B.A.). It is not known if Monet's wife had a profession before he met her, but her elegance in pose and dress makes one wonder if she might have been a seamstress or otherwise involved in the fashion industry. Her stylishness was such that other artists such as Pierre-Auguste Renoir and Manet wanted to paint her. It is not too unrealistic to conclude that painters of this time stretched the conventional boundaries of art to accommodate the spirit of the modern women they knew so intimately.

Since the early days of French Impressionism were so marked by the free-wheeling New Woman as she was defined at mid-century, it should come as no surprise that the commission for a mural to be entitled *Modern Woman* for the Chicago world's fair of 1893 should be awarded to the Impressionist Mary Cassatt. The mural, along with its counterpart, *Primitive Woman*, was to decorate the barrel-vaulted Hall of Honor inside the Woman's Building, the most elaborate pavilion ever dedicated to the accomplishments of women in a world's fair before or since. The erection of the building and the selection of its decorations and exhibitions were overseen by Bertha Honoré Palmer, president of the Board of Lady Managers for the building. For the visual arts she relied heavily on Sarah Hallowell, who had organized art exhibitions for previous fairs. They went to Paris to name a muralist for the building because the most accomplished American women artists were working in Paris at that time. After being turned down by Elizabeth Gardner, the dean of American women painters in Paris, they then approached Mary Fairchild MacMonnies, a rising young star in her early thirties who had married the equally successful young sculptor Frederick MacMonnies. It was resolved that MacMonnies, although she by right should have represented the most modern woman, would paint *Primitive Woman*, and Mary Cassatt, approaching fifty, would paint *Modern Woman*.[9]

Although it is clear that Cassatt's composition was more modern than MacMonnies's pastiche of classical and Italian Renaissance motifs, it is surprising that Cassatt shows us a different face of the modern woman than she had ten years before. Instead of the defiant, self-absorbed women of the 1860s and 1870s, the modern woman of the nineties was larger, more earnest, and more willing to show a "public" face. Like the middle-aged Cassatt the modern woman had responsibilities to her family and to society. The central panel, which Cassatt described as "Young women plucking the fruits of knowledge or science,"[10] (Fig. 4) pays homage to women's education, which had seen great progress in the last half of the nineteenth century, particularly with the opening of most of the major American women's colleges, including Mount Holyoke (1837), Vassar (1865), Smith (1875), Wellesley (1875), Bryn Mawr (1880), Goucher (1885), and Randolph-Macon Woman's College (1891). The women pluck the fruits of knowledge not only for themselves, but are shown passing them on to the younger generation. This theme, with its acknowledgment of broader public responsibility, differs from the modern woman of Cassatt's youth who was often seen reading newspapers and novels solely for her own benefit. The new

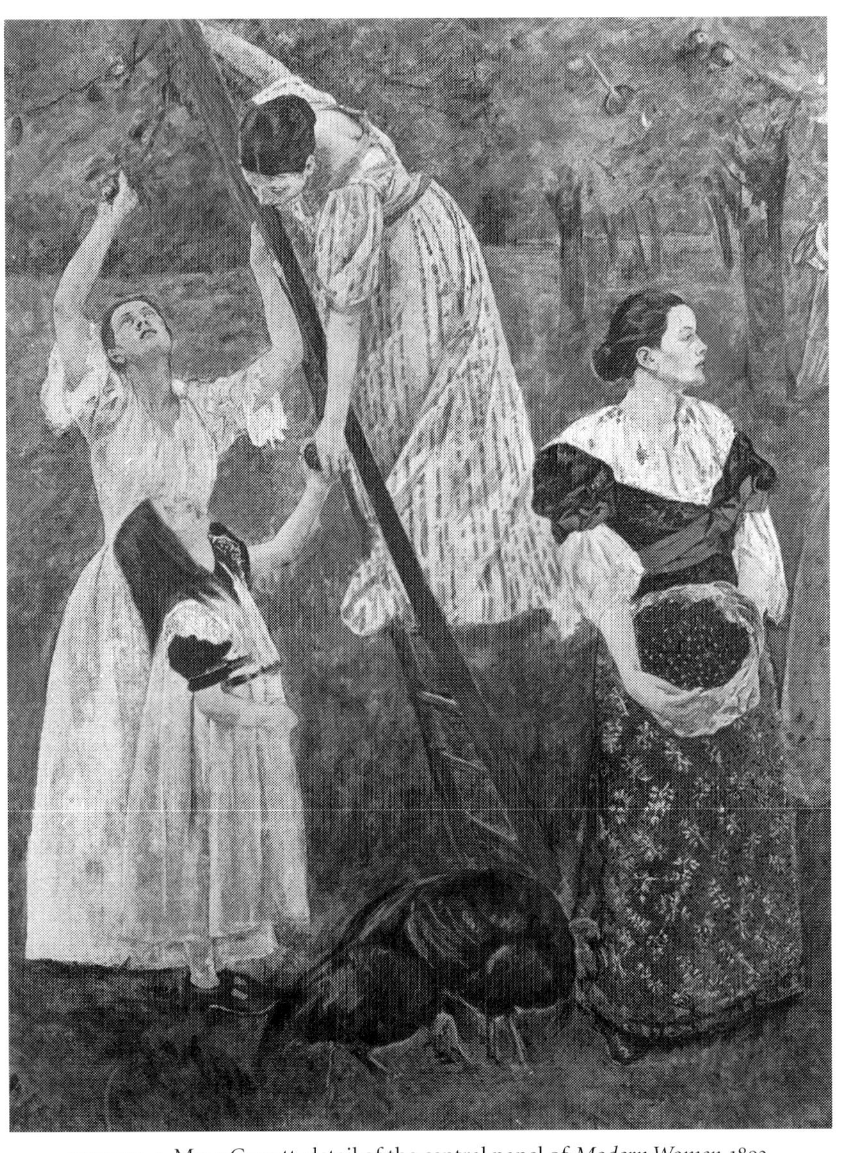

FIGURE 4 Mary Cassatt, detail of the central panel of *Modern Women*, 1893.

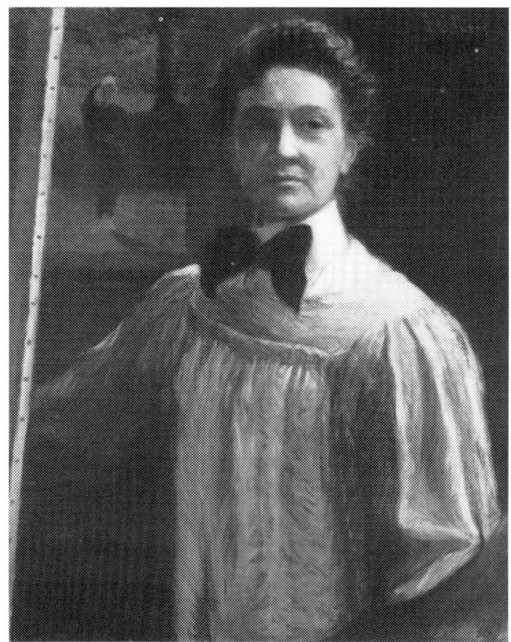

FIGURE 5 Lilla Cabot Perry,
Self-Portrait, 1891.
Oil on canvas. Daniel J. Terra
Collection.

modern woman took her role seriously. The critic André Mellério wrote about one of Cassatt's women in the mural as having "the grandeur and simplicity of a young priestess in an antique procession."[11] The mood of the *Modern Woman* mural parallelled symbolist interests, which had displaced Impressionist naturalism in the 1880s, and resonated with Cassatt's new symbolist theme, the mother and child.

The modern woman at the end of the nineteenth century was still very likely to turn to the arts for an income, in spite of the many other occupations and professions that had opened up to women in preceding decades.[12] Moreover, the face of the modern woman in the nineties was very likely to be a serious self-portrait, such as Lilla Cabot Perry's *Self-Portrait* of 1891 (Terra Museum of American Art, Fig. 5). Perry, four years younger than Cassatt, was exactly the kind of woman who was entering the art field at this time. She began her studies in her late thirties after marrying and having three children. She was socially prominent and inherited a small amount of money—enough to allow her to put in the years of study necessary before she could begin to sell her paintings. Her husband was a writer and academic whose income was fairly low. As a family, they counted on the addition of Mrs. Perry's art sales and commissions.

When Perry began to study in Europe, she gravitated toward the Impressionist style, which to her represented greater freedom and a respect for the modern woman.[13] In 1889 she visited an exhibition of Monet's work in Paris and subsequently took her family to spend the summer in Giverny. She returned to Giverny nine times in the next two decades and became close friends with Monet and the American painters of his circle at Giverny. Back home in Boston she promoted Monet and Impressionism and was active in a number of artists' associations. Perry represents the seriousness with which women pursued both their careers as artists and their responsibilities to family and community.

Unfortunately, because of the popularity of art as a career for women and the rising popularity of Impressionism, the serious women who thought they had "arrived" when the Woman's Building opened in 1893, soon began to feel the sting of a backlash. In Giverny alone, Monet and his fellow male artists retreated from the numerous women who arrived in the small town in the early 1890s. The American artist Will Low remembered that his friend Theodore Robinson

> contritely owned partial responsibility for the feminine invasion, as he had unguardedly recommended the place to one or two young women painters in Paris. Next to Monet, he was, indeed, the painter they most looked up to, all these numerous and charming would-be impressionists; but he was so ungallant as to shun their society, having a room in the village, away from the hotel, deserting the table d'hôte, and taking his meals in the little cafe fronting on the street, which, serving as a drinking place for the peasants, was comparatively free from the invasion of the gentler sex. . . .
>
> In another year or two the sudden wave of popularity deserted Giverny, and the bevy of student-esses deserted the meadows, and the hill slope saw them no longer . . .[14]

Will Low's thinly veiled contempt for the modern women artists of the 1890s is indicative of the cold shoulder that women began to get after they showed their numbers and their seriousness in such diverse sites as the Chicago world's fair and Giverny. Mary Cassatt's mural of the modern woman was soundly criticized for its jarring color and its seemingly obscure symbolism. As a result, she, like the women at Giverny, began to retreat and capitulate to the demands for prettier subjects and less demanding allusions to the modern woman. In the later 1890s she turned to charming pastels of women and children in playful or anecdotal poses.

Cassatt's retreat ameliorated those critics who wished for a less realistic and more pleasing "face" for the modern woman. After 1900, even though she continued to explore the monumental mother and child, she chose more attractive models and winsome children and babies. The result was an increase in her sales and a boom in her popularity, particularly in her own country. A painting like *The Caress*, 1903 (National Museum of American Art, Fig. 6), won the Walter Lippincott Prize when it was shown at the Pennsylvania Academy of the Fine Arts in 1904 and the Norman Wait Harris Prize at the Art Institute of Chicago later that same year. As one critic put it:

> *The Caress* was certainly one of her most beautiful examples, since she has deferred on this occasion to popular prejudice as to choose types of humanity that are not positively disconcerting in their homeliness. As a result, there is nothing to interfere with our enjoyment of her mastery of composition and drawing, of tone and light-ing. It is truly a lovely canvas![15]

She tasted the success that she and so many other modern women sought but found nearly impossible to attain. By 1910 she was called "The Most Eminent Living American Woman Painter"[16] and began to think her art might actually make her rich.[17]

Her success and her prominence in the art press brought that most sincere form of flattery—imitation—as can be seen in a work like Agnes Millen Rich-mond's *Mother and Child* of 1907 (Collection of Dr. and Mrs. J. T. Cooper, fig. 7). When Cassatt grew irritated at critics who claimed she copied Degas, she would retort to her friends that *she* was the one who was always being copied: "I cannot open a catalogue without seeing stealings from me."[18] Her famous mother and child compositions were copied by male and female artists alike for several decades into the twentieth century and can be detected even today in the work of some popular portraitists. Although she expressed awareness of her im-itators, she never objected to them. In fact, she was always willing to receive the many artists and art students who came to her door. She would patiently look at their portfolios and encourage them to work hard. While she never took on reg-ular students, she was interested in promoting their progress and sometimes recommended teachers to them. After 1900 she became associated with the Art League, an organization for American art students connected with the Hostel for American Students in Paris. She spoke to the group frequently and estab-lished a scholarship for two women students to spend a year in St. Quentin where they could study the pastels of seventeenth- and eighteenth-century mas-ters. Like the women in her *Modern Woman* mural, she wanted to hand down the "fruits from the tree of knowledge" to the younger generation.

In the years after the turn of the century, she found that her idea of the duties and responsibilities of the modern woman were not always those of the women who were like grandchildren to her. Their badges of modernity seemed so dif-

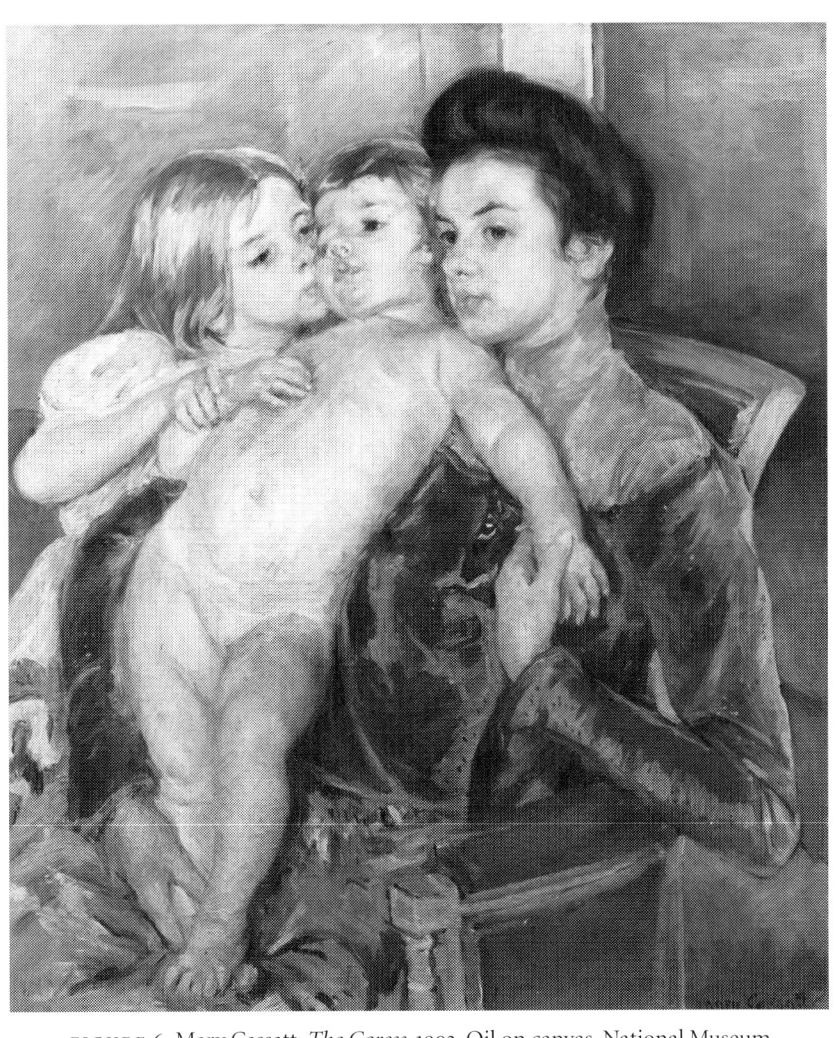

FIGURE 6 Mary Cassatt, *The Caress*, 1902. Oil on canvas. National Museum of American Art, Smithsonian Institution, gift of William T. Evans.

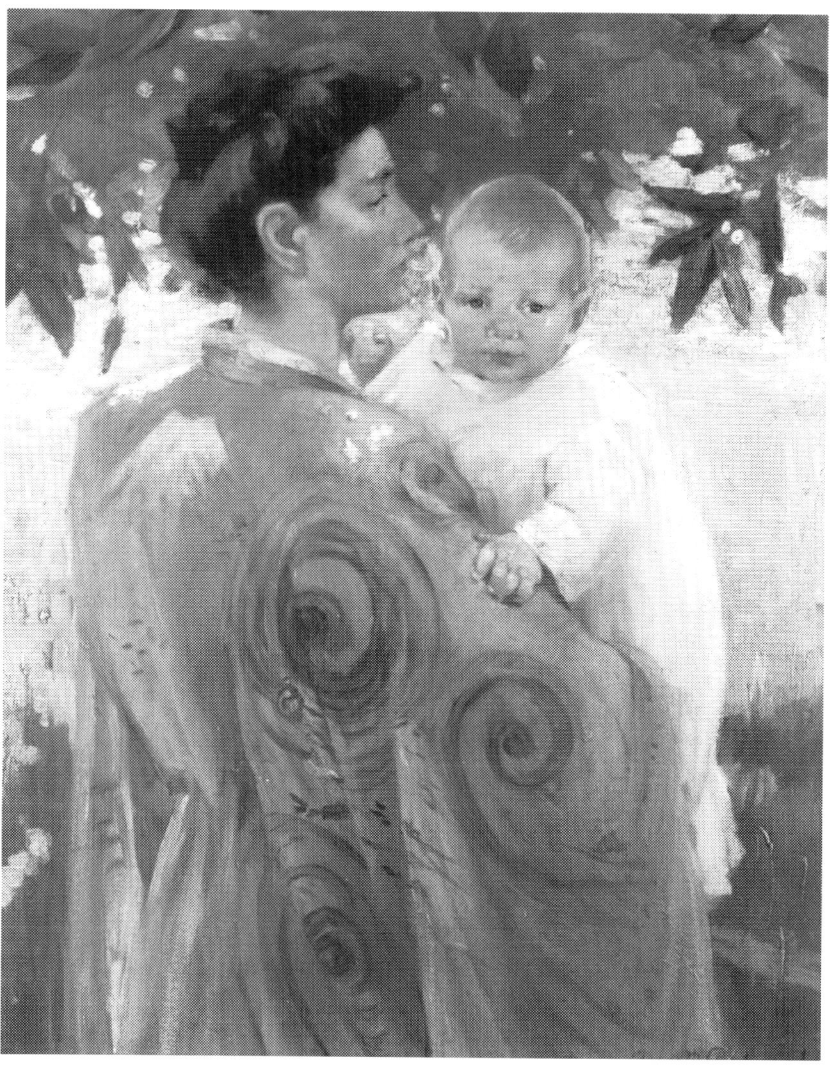

FIGURE 7 Agnes Millen Richmond, *Mother and Child*, 1907. Oil on canvas.
Collection of Dr. and Mrs. J.T. Cooper.

ferent from hers—even those she had worn as a young woman. Her young nieces, Ellen Mary and Eugenia, were ambitious and talked of going into business, but they shied away from education and travel and, like the teenagers they were, prided themselves on such scandalous behavior as smoking. As Cassatt wrote to her friend Louisine Havemeyer:

Here is Eugenia smoking (all Ellen's friends smoke) & their Mother has succeeded in making them promise not to smoke more than *three* times a day! and only *at home*. There is no harm in a woman smoking if she is careful not to oversmoke, but a girl not yet sixteen! and Ellen only nineteen. I wrote to Jennie to say that it would be good for Eugenia to profit by this coming winter spent in Paris to study languages, she says I am an artist, but she is just a 20th Century girl.[19]

Eugenia had the same reckless, defiant spirit of every new generation, but the smallness of her goals was shocking to her aunt. Neither Renée Mauperin nor Jo March would have passed up such an opportunity to study languages in a foreign country, nor would the young Cassatt or Morisot have done so.

Cassatt's disappointment with her nieces turned to bitterness when she learned that they, along with Cassatt's two sisters-in-law, had become active in the anti-suffrage movement in the United States. Cassatt had long been pro-suffrage and had recently become more intimately involved in the workings of the suffrage movement through her good friend Louisine Havemeyer, an organizer of the annual New York marches for suffrage sponsored by the Women's Political Union. Havemeyer had held exhibitions of her famous art collection to benefit the movement in the past, and in 1915 persuaded Cassatt to consent to an exhibition with Degas which would serve the same purpose. Cassatt became so involved in the effort—her first taste of political organizing—that she was unprepared for the opposition that was inevitably mounted against the exhibition. It was shunned by New York society as well as by the contingent of Philadelphia society—her own family—which normally would have been in attendance. The clash between Cassatt and her family over the issue of suffrage caused irreparable damage to their previously close relationship. Cassatt proved herself to be more modern than the "twentieth-century girls" who were her nieces.

In one regard, however, Cassatt was not more modern than the women who opposed her in the younger generation. This was in the matter of the modernist evolution toward increasingly abstract art. If the women in Matisse's paintings, such as *Blue Nude*, 1907 (Baltimore Museum of Art) showed the new face of the modern woman, Cassatt did not want to see it. She believed that the thirst for notoriety drove artists like Matisse and collectors like the Steins to perpetuate

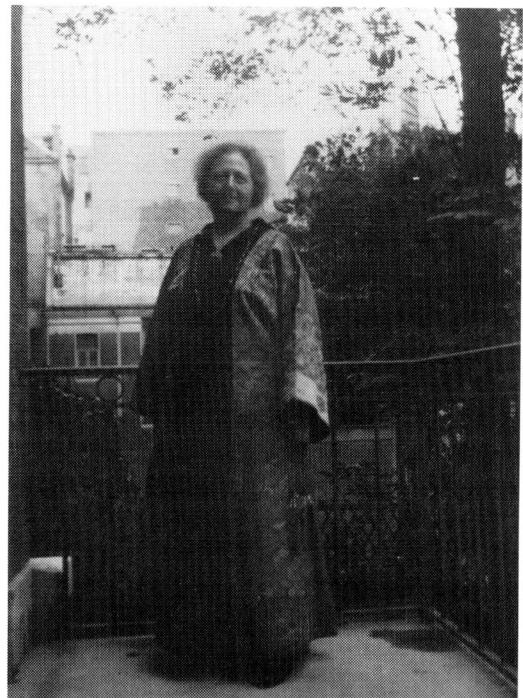

FIGURE 8 Sarah Stein, Paris, 1934. Baltimore Museum of Art, Cone Archives.

meaningless styles like these ("No sound artist ever looked except with scorn at these cubists and Matisse"[20]). Cassatt lumped the new women who supported this art, such as Gertrude Stein, her friends the Cone sisters (one of whom was a medical doctor), and her sister-in-law Sarah Stein, with her misguided nieces, but considered their efforts more publicly daring. Unlike the women of Cassatt's generation who used their physicality to "turn their backs" (Fig. 7) on the viewer in an effort to create their own psychological space, Cassatt felt that the women of this new generation used their physicality to invite the viewer to intrude. She told the story of how Michael and Sarah Stein would dress for their parties: "Stein received in sandals and his wife in one garment fastened by a brooch, which if it gave way might disclose the costume of Eve. Of course the curiosity was aroused and the anxiety as to whether it *would* give way . . . ."[21] (Fig. 8) She was so angered by the support these women gave to what she considered an unworthy modern art that she could not begin to appreciate their contributions in other ways. It seems that she was ignorant of Gertrude Stein's writing and other modernist literature of her day.

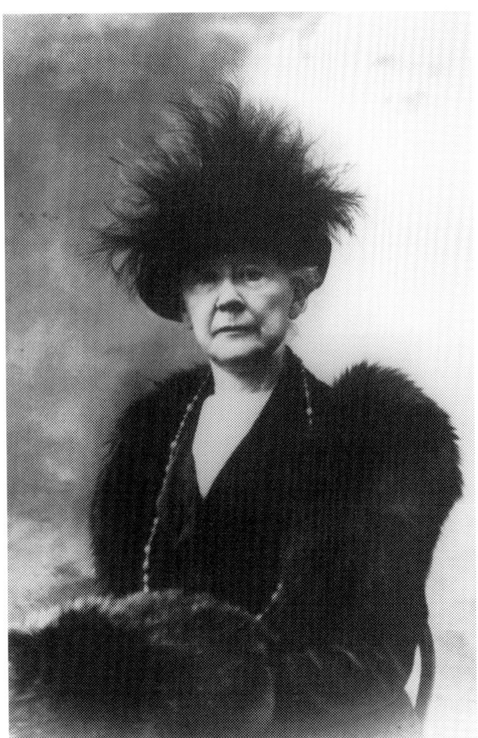

FIGURE 9 Mary Cassatt, 1914.
Archives of American Art,
Smithsonian Institution.

In spite of her opposition to the new movements, Cassatt was firm in her belief that art should not be bound and confined. She refused to serve on exhibition juries and wrote passionately to convince others to drop the system altogether. As she wrote to the director of fine arts of the Carnegie Institute in Pittsburgh:

I have never served because I could never reconcile it to my conscience to be the means of shutting the door in the face of a fellow painter. I think the jury system may lead, & in the case of the Exhibitions at the Carnegie Institute no doubt does lead to a high average, but in art what we want is the certainty that the one spark of original genius shall not be extinguished, that is better than average excellence, that is what will survive, what it is essential to foster.[21]

Whether she recognized that her modern philosophy led to the art she deplored is not important. What is important is that the face that she showed to the world, as weary as it became in old age, was always what she believed to be the face of the modern woman (Fig. 9).

NOTES

1   This contextual approach to the figure was at the heart of the Impressionist aesthetic and was eloquently summed up by Edmond Duranty in his 1876 pamphlet, The New Painting: "Farewell to the human body treated like a vase . . . what we need is the particular note of the modern individual, in his clothing, in the midst of his social habits . . . .By means of a back, we want a temperament, an age, a social condition to be revealed; through a pair of hands, we should be able to express a magistrate or a tradesman; by a gesture, a whole series of feelings . . . ." Quoted in *Impressionism and Post-Impressionism 1874-1904 Sources and Documents*, Linda Nochlin, ed. (Englewood Cliffs: Prentice Hall, 1966), 5.

2   Jules and Edmond de Goncourt, *Renée Mauperin*, trans. Alys Hallard (New York: D. Appleton & Co., 1902), 44-45.

3   Quotations from Morisot's notebook, c. 1895, as cited in Anne Higonnet, *Berthe Morisot* (New York: Harper & Row, 1990), 3.

4   Louisa May Alcott, *Little Women* (New York: Penguin Books, 1989), 147.

5   Mary Haldeman to Eliza Haldeman, 18 December 1866, Private Collection.

6   Eliza Haldeman to Samuel Haldeman, 26 January 1861, Pennsylvania Academy of the Fine Arts. For Cassatt's feminist context during her student days, see the author's biography, *Mary Cassatt: A Life* (New York: Villard Books, 1994), 19-20.

7   For a discussion of this development in England, see Paula Gillett, *Worlds of Art* (New Brunswick: Rutgers University Press, 1990), especially Chapter 5 "Painting and the Independent Woman."

8   Nathaniel Hawthorne, *The Marble Faun* (New York: Penguin Books, 1990), 54-55.

9   Mary Fairchild MacMonnies apparently chose to do "the more romantic *Primitive Woman*." Although she had done portraits in an Impressionist style, her most recent project had been to copy Botticelli's frescoes in a Florentine villa, indicating her interest in Old Masters and the antique. See Mary Smart, "Sunshine and Shade: Mary Fairchild MacMonnies Low," *Woman's Art Journal* 4, 2 (Fall 1983/Winter 1984): 22.

10   Mary Cassatt to Bertha Palmer, October 11 [1892], Art Institute of Chicago.

11   André Mellério, Preface to *Exposition Mary Cassatt* (Paris: Durand Ruel Galleries, 1893), n.p.

12   In the popular women's employment guide *What Can a Woman Do?* by Martha L. Rayne (1893, reprinted Arno Press, 1974), the professions of literature, journalism, music, wood engraving, and industrial arts make up about twenty percent of the fields listed in the table of contents (which also include law, medicine, secretarial, dressmaking, and agricultural pursuits). Although not listed in the table of contents, architecture and fine arts are also covered in the text.

13   Perry's understanding of Monet and Impressionism was typical of the small group of Americans who discovered the style in the late 1880s: "Monet's philosophy of painting was to paint what you really see, not what you ought to see; not the object enveloped in sunlight and atmosphere, with the blue dome of Heaven reflected in the shadows."

"Reminiscences of Claude Monet From 1889 to 1909" (1927) reprinted in *Lilla Cabot Perry: An American Impressionist* (Washington, DC: National Museum of Women in the Arts, 1990), 116. She appreciated and tried to duplicate his images of women as "you really see [them]." She also admired and became friendly with the women of the French Impressionist group, Mary Cassatt and Berthe Morisot.

14 Will H. Low, *Chronicles of Friendship* (1908), 446f as quoted in David Sellin, *Americans in Brittany and Normandy, 1860-1910,*(Phoenix: Phoenix Art Museum, 1982), 68-69.

15 Charles H. Caffin, "American Studio Talk: Pennsylvania Academy Exhibition," *International Studio* (March 1904): 239.

16 "The Most Eminent of Living American Women Painters," *Current Literature* (February 1909): 167.

17 Mary Cassatt's fortune in 1910 might be estimated at about $200,000, which was enough for her to maintain an apartment in Paris, a country house at Mesnil-Théribus, and a rented villa in Grasse near Cannes; however, it was paltry compared to the $50 million estimated to have been left by her brother Alexander upon his death in 1906.

18 Mary Cassatt to Louisine Havemeyer, 12 March [1915], Metropolitan Museum of Art.

19 Mary Cassatt to Louisine Havemeyer, 16 July [1913], Metropolitan Museum of Art.

20 Mary Cassatt to Ellen Mary Cassatt, 26 March [1913?], Philadelphia Museum of Art.

21 Mary Cassatt to John W. Beatty, 5 September [1905], Archives of American Art.

The American Personality in the Age of American Impressionism

SARAH BURNS

———

IN 1892, William Howe Downes, critic for the *Boston Evening Transcript*, reviewed an exhibition by local artists at the St. Botolph Club. Noting the predominance of portraits in this show, along with a remarkable array of Impressionist landscapes, he paused to wonder about the expediency of exhibiting portraits of "private personages" in public shows, since, in his view, such works could not possibly have the general interest which a few "ideal canvases" would have provided. So overwhelming were these painted effigies that they prompted Downes to complain about the "almost oppressive" sensation they produced, these excessively numerous tableaux depicting self-conscious people sitting about in their best clothes, wondering why they were there. At the same time, however, he acknowledged that there was something "intensely modern" about these works, which, like the Impressionist landscapes in the Georgia Museum of Art's exhibition, were loosely executed and full of vivacity. Downes attributed this modern style to the impact of American expatriate John Singer Sargent, who having very recently concluded in 1890 his second resoundingly successful portrait-painting sweep of major Eastern cities, had established himself as a vivid presence in contemporary American portraiture. The sources of the "intensely modern" mode of portrait painting were in fact somewhat more diverse, comprising aspects of the Munich style best represented by Frank Duveneck and William Merritt Chase and the bold, energetic productions of the popular Swedish master Anders Zorn and the Italian Giovanni Boldini, two among several European specialists who reaped abundant commissions to paint prominent Americans in the late nineteenth century. Certainly French Impressionism itself had played a role in defining that clever, dashing style Downes associated with Sargent. In the late 1880s, his interest piqued by the *plein air* work of his friend Claude Monet, Sargent had executed a number of outdoor portraits, casually posed and brightly colored, featuring figures fully integrated with and even absorbed into the surrounding light and atmosphere. Numerous American painters engaged in similar ventures in the 1890s and beyond, creating radiant modern visions of healthy bodies in the vibrant, open air.[1]

Equally prevalent, though, were more ambitious, prestigious portraits, formal yet lively, which attempted a new fusion of the traditional, monumental portrait format with the modern pursuit of optical sensation, nervous force, and personal expression. As Michael Quick has observed, the dominant and very serviceable style of the 1870s and 1880s had tended to be fashioned after dramatic realism, as in Cecilia Beaux's *Les Derniers jours d'enfance* [*The Last Days of Infancy*] (1883-85, Pennsylvania Academy of the Fine Arts, Philadelphia), which shows a mingling of fellow Philadelphian Thomas Eakins's moody concreteness and shadowy hues with the decorative posing of James McNeill Whistler, another potent force in the shaping of late nineteenth-century portrait styles. But by the 1890s, after a period of study in Paris, Beaux, like numerous contemporaries, had shifted to a technique featuring light, movement, and glistening surfaces, as in the portrait of her brother-in-law *Henry Drinker*, 1898 (Fig. 1), a dazzling study in whites which looks back to Whistler's *Symphony in White No. 1: The Little White Girl* (1862, National Gallery of Art, Washington, DC). With numerous personal variations, such a style, compounded of diverse ingredients, was to define the most fashionable mode of society portrait throughout the American *fin de siècle* and into the early decades of the twentieth century.[2]

The commanding status of portraits noted at the St. Botolph Club exhibition by Downes was symptomatic of a pervasive interest in the genre that continued through the 1890s and beyond. Considering this strong and persistent presence, late nineteenth-century portraiture and its social functions demand further exploration. What factors contributed to the well-documented popularity and ubiquity of the prestigious society portrait in the period under review? The National Academy of Design alone sponsored a number of successful loan exhibitions of portraits in 1894, 1895, 1898, and 1903, each time to considerable acclaim and substantial attendance.[3] On a mass-media level the emerging, popular, middle-class magazines of the 1890s both catered to and helped create a rage for portraits in a wide variety of forms, from reproductions of paintings to drawings, prints, and photographs. Their mass circulation greatly facilitated by the rise of new photomechanical techniques for reproduction, portraits in magazines displayed to a growing audience models of style, celebrity, power, and achievement in society, business, art, and war. In monetary terms the currency

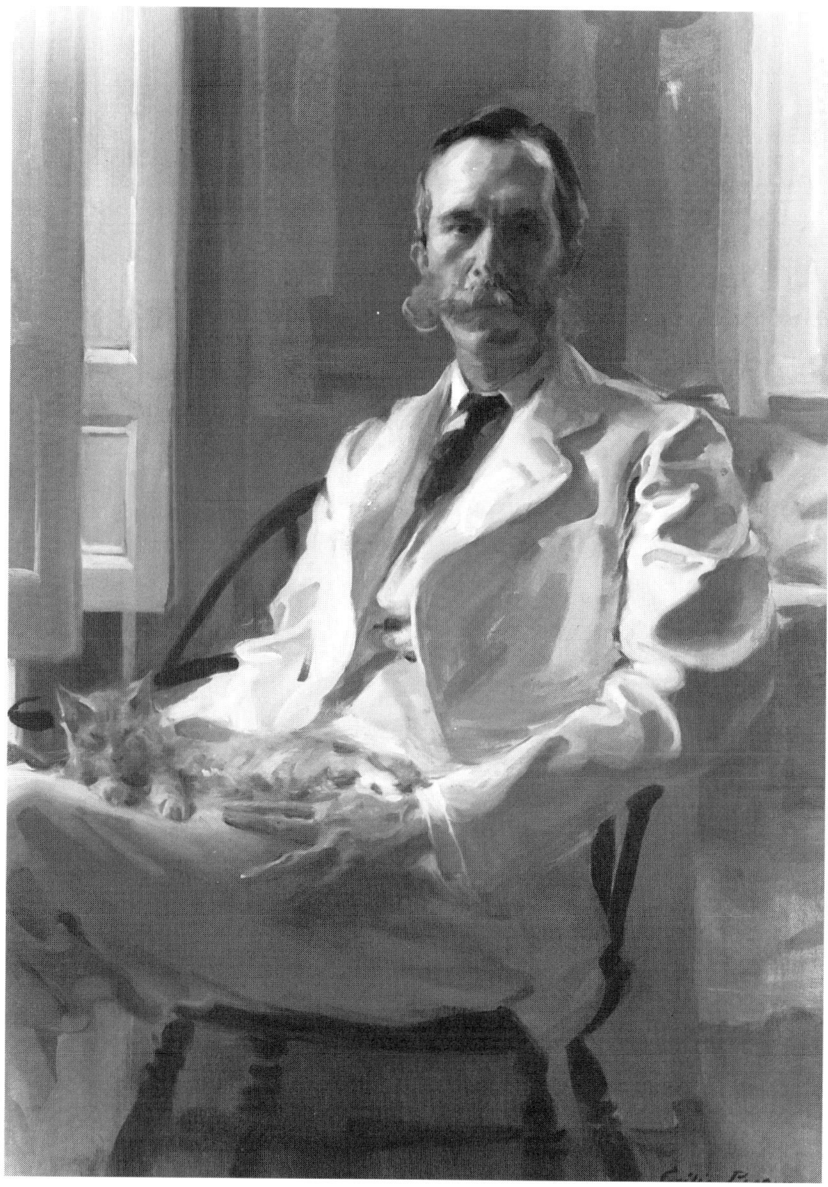

FIGURE 1 Cecilia Beaux, *Man With the Cat (Henry Sturgis Drinker)*. 1898. Oil on canvas. National Museum of American Art, Smithsonian Institution, bequest of Henry Ward Ranger through the National Academy of Design.

of portraits ran high; artists in demand, such as Sargent and Boldini, could receive many thousands of dollars for a single painting.[4] What was it about portraits that appealed to the American public, and to what extent did they contribute to the shaping of public notions about what constituted nationality, cultivation, and success? In what ways did they affirm, transform, or blur the relation between the public and private self? How did they fit into and spring from the never-stable and often anxious social texture of the time? While each individual case possessed its own unique properties, many of the portraits produced by and for Americans around the turn of the century embodied current and often conflicting answers to such questions.

By the later decades of the nineteenth century, outward appearance and behavior came increasingly to be equated with who a person was, displacing older notions of inner character as the true index of worth. Industrial capitalism, which replaced local production and hand labor with mass production and distribution that simultaneously alienated worker from product and created a vast new world of goods, was instrumental in effecting this displacement. It also created the consumer culture that emerged both because of and in response to the marketplace, where an endless array of commodities promised to sate the boundless desires generated by material abundance. As smaller, self-contained communities steadily lost ground to the power of the urban sphere where masses of strangers daily encountered each other, appearances as a means of announcing and decoding the individual assumed increasing importance. In response, social performance and the concept of the self defined by consumption—colors selected, ornaments chosen, taste in wallpaper and bric-a-brac— became the vehicles by which status and personality communicated themselves. Richard Sennett has noted that the rise of nineteenth-century secularism assisted in this process of change by exalting the reality of immediate sensation, immediate fact, and immediate feeling, which meant that "appearances in public, no matter how mystifying, still had to be taken seriously, because they might be clues to the person hidden behind the mask."[5] In the later decades of the century, individuality experienced the remorseless threat of suppression by the encroaching corporate organization, which reduced people to insignificant and even interchangeable parts in a vast, bureaucratic machine, depriving them of will and initiative. The cult of the unique personality, defined and distinguished by outward signs, gained vigor in the face of imminent eclipse and swelled the tide of obsession with portraits in all their forms during the American *fin de siècle*. As one critic of the trend complained:

Take up almost any periodical . . . , and you will find names, names, names; faces, faces, faces. There are many publications that enjoy wide circulation wholly through catering to the hunger for personalities . . . . Persons of unusual gifts and staying power are kept standing in type. Any individual who, by accident or unusual opportunity, is connected with an event of note, is trumpeted and thrown upon the screen.

Both men of genius and "the hero of the hour" enjoyed the dubious glare of the spotlight of what this writer called "anthropomania."[6]

Artists cultivated distinctive appearances and devised attention-getting personality traits for themselves as competitive strategies in an art market becoming increasingly free and commercial; personal styles in self and product were alike commodified, becoming in a sense trademarks that were vigorously promoted. Nowhere was concern with image-making more obsessive than in the case of Whistler, whose portrait painted by William Merritt Chase in London (1885, Metropolitan Museum of Art) dramatically displays the figure that appeared countless times in paintings, photographs, and caricature. The white lock, the monocle, the slim walking-stick, and the mannered pose, are all rendered, moreover, in the flattened, muted style of the expatriate master himself. Notwithstanding the fact that Whistler quite violently detested Chase's portrait as a caricature of his trademark eccentricities, the painting shrewdly reproduces precisely those elements that made up Whistler's self-created public image.[7] In turn, the cosmopolitan Sargent's portrait of Chase (Fig. 2) highlights the energy, masculinity, and authority that made up Chase's public persona, along with the style of dress that combined the crisp tailoring of the man-about-town with signs denoting allowable artistic eccentricity: the monocle, the bristling moustache, and the van Dyke beard.

Paradoxically, photographic literalism, the impartial recording of outward signs and surfaces, fell short of satisfying the desire to know the person. Indeed, the camera, as Homer St.-Gaudens put it, was likely to reproduce a person in an attitude or expression "false to his true self." Mechanical exactitude might mislead, he said, but "the personality of the artist" counted in portraiture, and achieved real power in combination with insight into the personality of the sitter. British aesthete Oscar Wilde had indicated as much early in the 1890s, when he pontificated that "the only portraits in which one believes are portraits where there is very little of the sitter and a very good deal of the artist."[8]

The question of just what was being truthfully displayed remained open, and it is clear that portraitists—even photographers—were expected to add value (whether in the form of their own personalities, or an enhanced and glamorized version of the sitter) to produce by public signs alone an impression of the real, inner, private person that the public, presumably, hungered to know and consume. The 1890 *Life* magazine cartoon by C. Carleton (Fig. 3) puts the situation

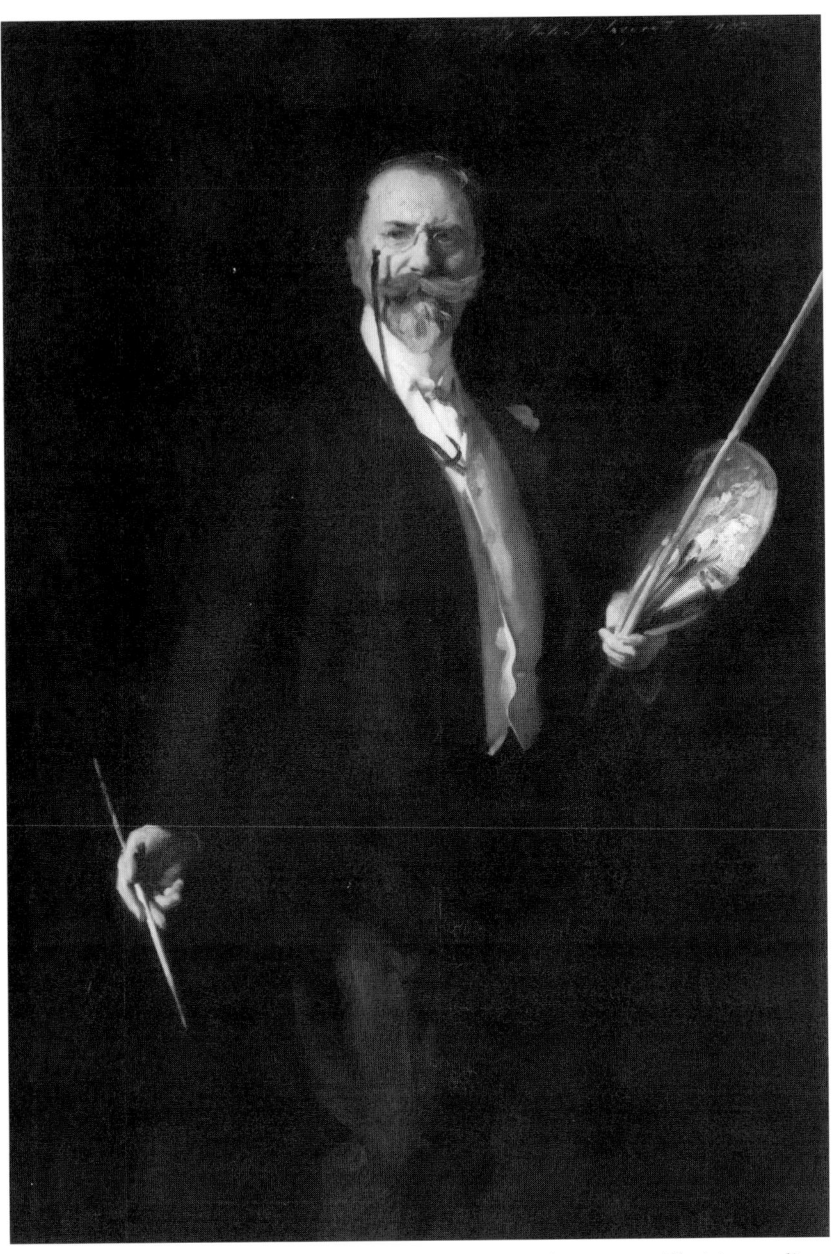

FIGURE 2 John Singer Sargent, *William Merritt Chase*. Oil on canvas. The Metropolitan Museum of Art, gift of the Pupils of William Merritt Chase, 1905.

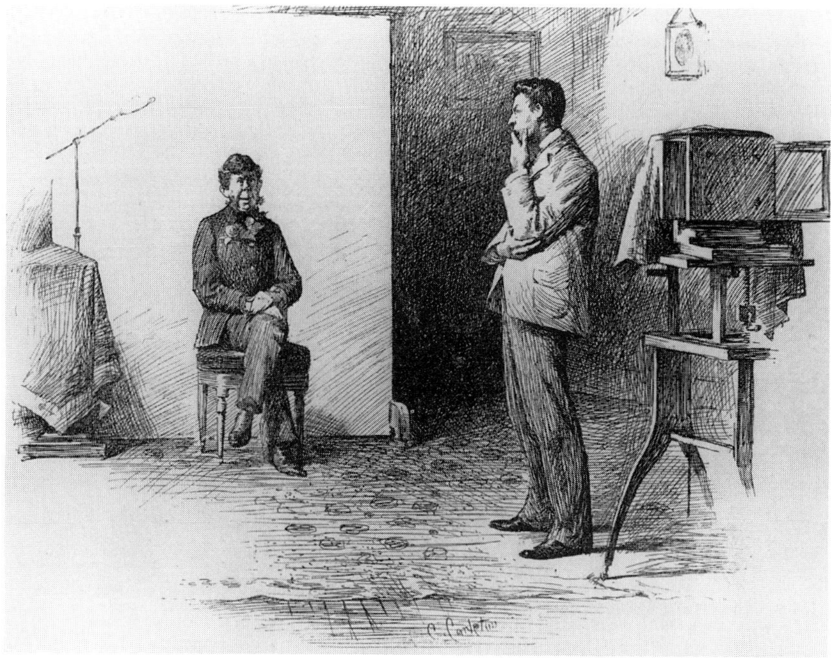

FIGURE 3 C. Carleton, *Too Strong A Resemblance,* October 2, 1890.
Cartoon. *Life* magazine, 16.

nicely; posing an undistinguished subject in front of the camera, the photographer, in a deliberative stance, suggests "Now try to look like yourself. [noting the effect]—Well, er, h–m; try to look like somebody else."[9] Later, *Munsey's Magazine,* in a feature significantly entitled "In the Public Eye," made sport of the same notion by contrasting a photograph of New York socialite Mrs. Burke Roche with her portrait painted by the fashionable foreigner Antonio de la Gandara (Fig. 4). Noting that whereas the pose in the painting coincided closely with that in the photograph, the caption observed wryly that feature, figure, and expression were "strangely different."[10] The painter had added a degree of style and verve not (at that time, at least) within the capabilities of photography. These surface qualities—optical impressions translated by personal touch into an image of lively chic—encode themselves as visual equivalents of the living personality, conveyed to us through the spirited posture, the theatrical hand-clasp, the cool yet alluring look, the delicately vibrant surfaces, the impression of gliding movement. Of course, no more than the photograph do these signs reveal the person within. The portrait shows us little more than a social mask,

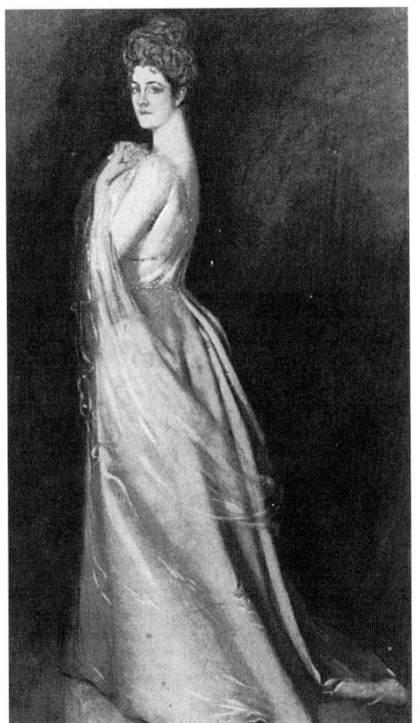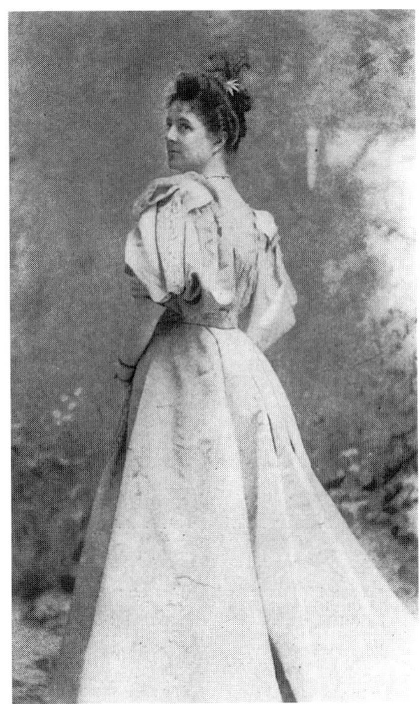

FIGURE 4 *"Look Here upon This Picture and on This"*, 1899. Reproduced cartoon. *Munsey's Magazine* February 20, 1899.

an aspect of the kind of elite social performance satirized so relentlessly by Thorstein Veblen in *Theory of the Leisure Class* of 1899. Yet because its surfaces betoken life, individuality, and momentariness, the image purports to give the knowledge-hungry public an intimate encounter with the essence of an authentic "personality," otherwise inaccessible through the boundaries of class and money. Indeed, such deviations from "truth" were not only tolerated but expected. As the *Boston Evening Transcript* said, "Everyone knows how Croesus, who made his money in pork and wishes us all to know that he did, and in Chicago, will depart unto Paris with a hard, shrewd face and a coarse and vulgar body, and yet return fetching a portrait that gives him a distinction that the noblest lord might covet . . . . Now, there is nothing so shameless as all this among the women's portraits at the Academy; but here and there a touch of matronly dignity or of girlish beauty brings surprise when one closely recalls the sitter."[11]

At the extreme, the sitter for a portrait could be subordinated to the painter's own personal and aesthetic imperatives and might serve (and often did, particularly in works by Whistler) as pretext for an arrangement, as in Chase's portrait of his student, Dora Wheeler (Fig. 5), who achieved moderate success as a painter and designer. Chase painted Wheeler in her own studio, sitting before a lush golden wall hanging (possibly produced by the design firm of her mother, Candace Wheeler) and surrounded by other luxurious furnishings. The portrait has been seen as the admiring tribute of one artist to another, and Dora Wheeler projects a compelling individuality. In the 1880s though, observers saw the work in quite different terms. When reviewing the Paris Salon of 1883, where *Dora Wheeler* was first exhibited, critic William Crary Brownell noted with distaste that the environment overwhelmed the figure: "Miss Wheeler counts for next to nothing in it, not only in lack of character . . . , but in point of pure pictorial relation to her surroundings." The next year, when the portrait appeared in New York at the Society of American Artists show, a critic in *The Nation* attacked its crude color along with the excessiveness of Chase's self-expression with palette knife, which seemed more like trowel and shovel work than painting. "It is the insanity of *chic*," fumed the reviewer, "sacrificing the real excellence of execution to the shallowest pedantry of the palette." Such criticisms again raise the issue of whose personality was on display. Brownell's curious findings aside, it is clear that anyone less angular and forceful than Dora Wheeler would have been badly vanquished by the riot of color and decoration into which Chase embedded her and through which he so vividly expressed his own sensuous responses to optical sensation, a capacity for which he received both praise (for being a "wonderful human camera") and blame (for the perceived inability to see beyond the surfaces of things).[12] It was this capacity, however, that made Chase's works distinctly contemporary. As one critic put it, "How splendidly he can paint! How he loves surfaces and caresses them with his brush! A brass vessel, a strip of gold plush . . . His talent is as superficial as it is brilliant. Perhaps this is an essential condition of artistic 'modernity' as of modern life."[13] Like Chase's brilliant still lifes, the modern portrait itself was to a large degree the product of a materialistic, consumeristic culture in which the lavish or restrained display of physical attributes and possessions summed up the nature and worth of the individual. The display of the well-tended body, decorated with tasteful and expensive things, was very much in tune with an era that both cultivated and deplored celebrity and self-advertisement.

Although critics often construed the work of Cecilia Beaux as sympathetic, intimate, and womanly, her ambitious public portraits well illustrate the materialistic tendency of so much *fin-de-siècle* portraiture. Beaux's *Mrs. Larz*

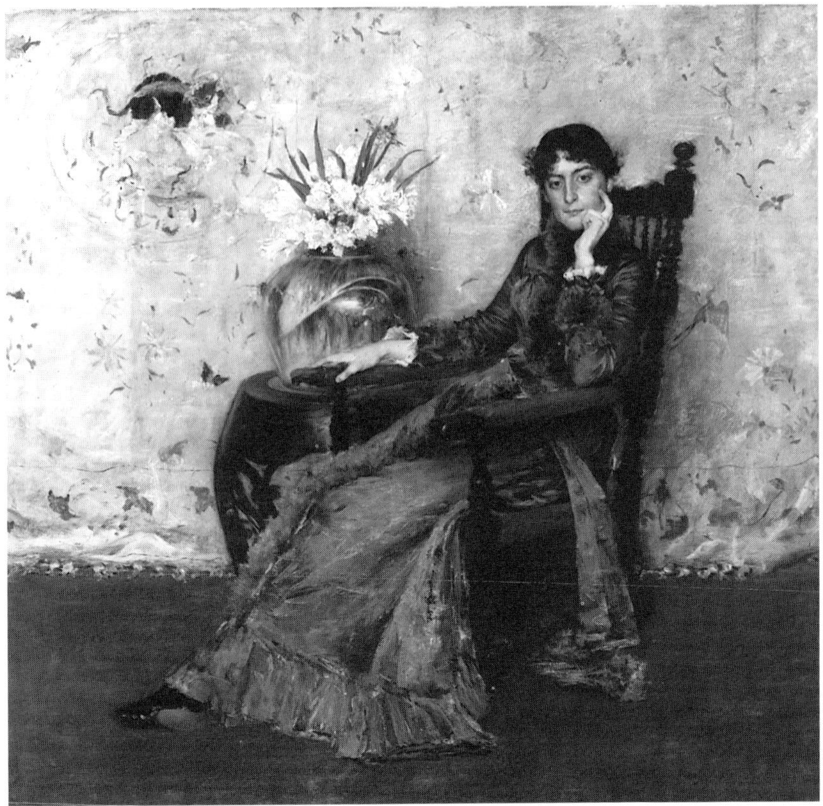

FIGURE 5 William Merritt Chase, *Portrait of Miss Dora Wheeler*, 1883. Oil on canvas.
The Cleveland Museum of Art, gift of Mrs. Boudinot Keith, in memory of
Mr. and Mrs. J. H. Wade.

Anderson (Fig. 6), exhibited in 1905 at the Pennsylvania Academy of the Fine
Arts, represents Isabel Perkins Anderson, the young yet impressively poised wife
of a noted diplomat, seen as if readying herself to receive guests in an opulent
home setting. The Philadelphia *Press* found that the portrait breathed "that air
of gorgeous surroundings, of much entertaining, of luxurious living among fine
bibelots and all the usual and cluttering *mise-en-scène* of our great houses."
Indeed, Mrs. Anderson's formidable presence prompted the *Press* to christen her
"The Hostess."[14] Here, obviously, only the public self was on view, a self almost
entirely characterized by expensive and tasteful trappings in an atmosphere of
wealth, privilege, and power. The novelist Willa Cather, who attended a dinner
party with Beaux on the occasion of the second annual Founders' Day prize cer-

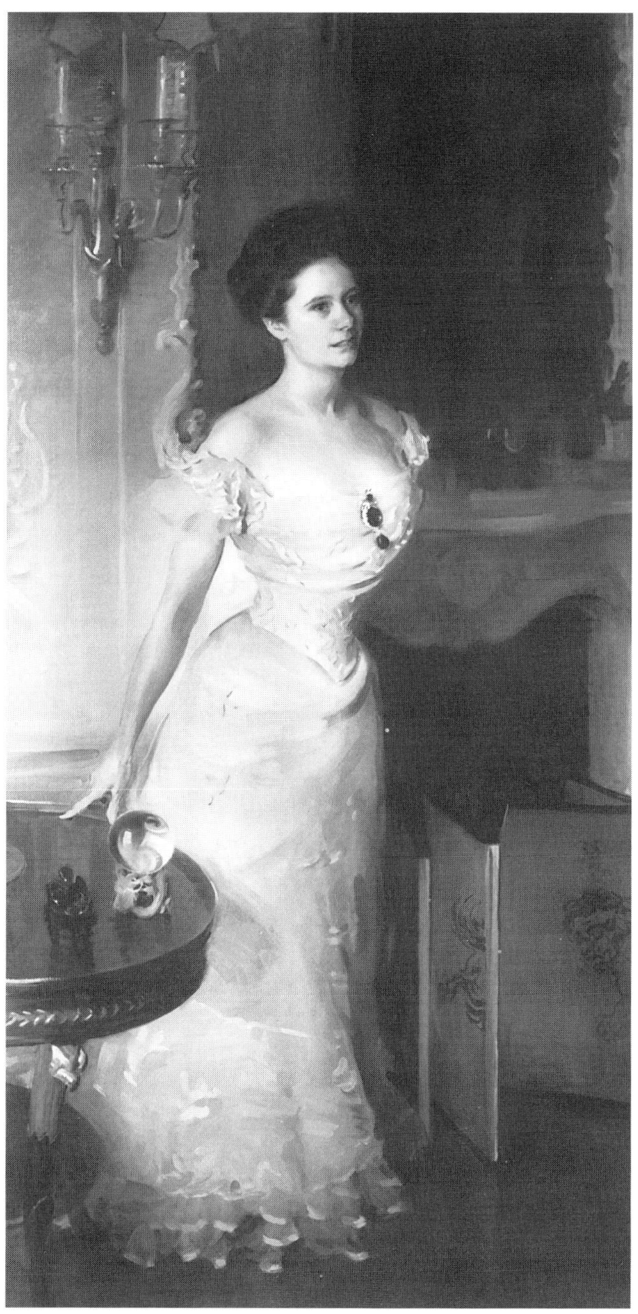

FIGURE 6 Cecilia Beaux, *Mrs. Larz Anderson*, 1900. Oil on canvas.
Anderson House Museum of the Society of the Cincinnati,
Washington, D.C.

emonies at the Carnegie Institute, also indicated her appreciation for the style and quality of things in Beaux's portraits when she remarked a bit snidely that "Cecilia Beaux's dinner gown deserves a whole *Courier*. She paints such pretty clothes, I wonder why she wears such awful ones."[15]

Sargent and other popular portrait painters likewise bore a certain degree of criticism directed against the superficiality of their descriptions. Critic Charles Caffin attributed this superficiality to the "excessive popularity of portraits of women of fashion, with all its temptations to the artist of pre-occupying himself with furbelows and finery in lieu of stronger and deeper qualities." The fact that Caffin saw this tendency in feminine portraits only indicates what Veblen already knew: that leisured women were the chief consumers in America's abundant marketplaces. Indeed, in the case of Sargent there was no agreement as to whether he was the most profound or the shallowest of observers, but no critic could discount the spectacular brio of his paintings. As Royal Cortissoz put it, Sargent's "restless brilliancy" was only the "natural expression of the leading traits in the world he depicts." He was "spectacular," a "giant," and "a type of materialism triumphant."[16] Sargent's *Mrs. Fiske Warren (Gretchen Osgood) and Her Daughter Rachel* (Fig. 7) bears Cortissoz out. Painted at Isabella Stewart Gardner's Fenway Court palace in Boston, the portrait shows mother and child arrayed in brilliant, almost frenzied cascades of shimmering, rippling, satiny and feathery textures, which set off their glowing, rose-leaf complexions, pellucid eyes, and amber waves of well-tended hair. Behind their throne-like seats glimmer the rich surfaces of Renaissance carvings and textiles. If there is anything psychological in the almost unsettling conjunction of the two heads or the awkward contrast of the mother's rigidly upright body with the daughter's pliant one, it is an open question whether these details express something profound about the relationship between woman and girl, or whether the painter arranged the pose to afford himself an acrobatic compositional challenge. In this case the "materialism triumphant" of Sargent's representation was a disappointment. Mrs. Warren felt—with considerable justification—that the artist had treated her as a "butterfly" and failed to illuminate any of the intellectual qualities in which she took pride.[17]

In one sense there was little radically new in the display of wealth and style that flaunted itself in so many turn-of-the-century portraits. Images of the powerful had nearly always symbolized status and authority through such means. Material display, however, took on new meanings and new energy in a modern consumerist society where an emerging advertising culture pervaded not simply the marketing of goods but the publicizing of individuals. In this development the mass media played a major role. Grown to unprecedented

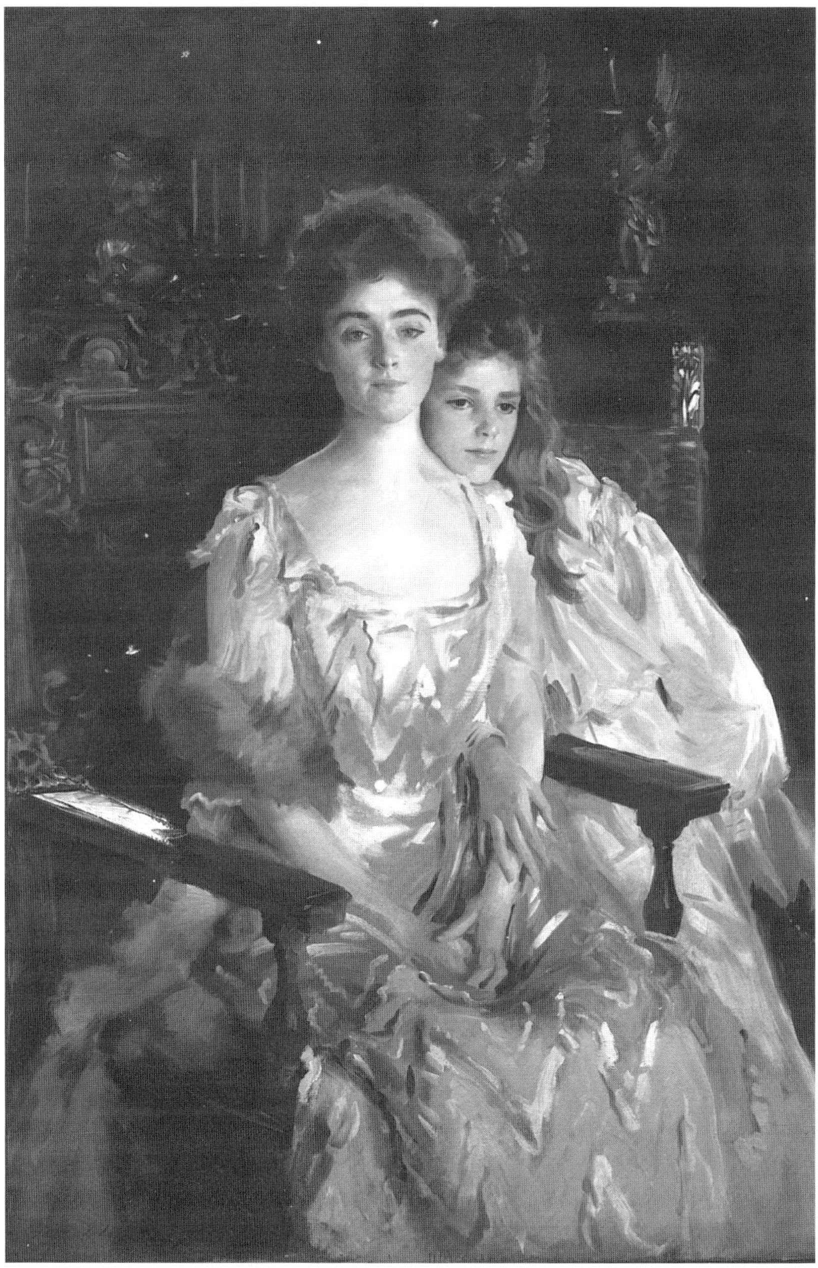

FIGURE 7 John Singer Sargent, *Mrs. Fiske Warren (Gretchen Osgood) and Her Daughter*, 1903. Oil on canvas. Museum of Fine Arts, Boston, gift of Mrs. Rachel Warren Barton and the Emily L. Ainsley Fund.

strength and proportions in the 1890s with the introduction of the ten-cent monthly which vastly increased the popular audience, the magazines mass-produced and distributed typeset and pictorial versions of life, news, and information about virtually every aspect of human society and culture, feeding this diet to voracious readers who consumed that week's menu and demanded more. The media in turn fed upon events, stories, and personalities in order to produce the next issue. This was precisely what concerned the novelist Henry James when he reflected on changes the rise of the popular press had brought about: ". . . it is possible among us to-day to become a celebrity on unprecedentedly easy terms . . . . It is more and more striking that the machinery of publicity is so enormous, so constantly growing, and so obviously destined to make the globe small . . . that it procures for the smallest facts and the most casual figures a reverberation to be expected only in the case of a world-conqueror."[18]

As James noted, anyone could achieve celebrity and briefly fuel the publicity machine. The vogue for portraits in the magazines of the 1890s was one consequence of the new cult of publicity, as was an obsession with personalities of every description: public and often private lives were commodified and offered up to hundreds of thousands of curious eyes. In the mid-1890s, an editorial in the *Century* professed bewilderment at the "craze for publicity." Why, demanded the writer, Richard Watson Gilder, did Americans have such a feverish urge to have their doings recorded in print and communicated to the public? "Why in the world should a man or woman care to advertise things which are not to be sold—a wedding trousseau, the decorations of a bedroom, a dinner to friends . . . . ? We can see well enough why a dealer in old silver should be pleased at having his wares described in the newspapers. But what interest has Mr. Newman Biggs in having the public made aware of the splendor and solidity of his plate?" While conceding that for artists and authors public life might be a necessary way of drawing attention to their productions, Gilder still could not imagine why people engaged in the ordinary round of existence "should wish to have their lives turned inside out on the newsstands."[19] The relation between individuals and the media was a self-producing, self-devouring loop, compounded of a desire to sell magazines and newspapers, an individual desire for notoriety, and individual satisfaction of displaying power and reinforcing social hierarchy, while at the same time fostering the illusion of democracy, since intimate details from the lives of the rich and powerful brought the ordinary reader into an imaginary (and very temporary) proximity with them. Alternatively, stories and pictures of material extravagance might lend a sense of empowerment to middle-class audiences, who could take advantage of the opportunity to deplore the frequent excesses of the very rich.

On a somewhat more exclusive level, society portraits in public exhibitions took on the same coloring of self-advertisement as did the doings of the wealthy that filled contemporary gossip columns, and the same class of cultural watchdog attacked them both. *Life* magazine quoted a daily paper on the attire of Mrs. Bradley Martin, gowned in "gorgeous" turquoise blue satin encrusted with jewels. It may be natural, said *Life*, to bedeck oneself with the contents of a jeweler's window and place oneself on exhibition, but it was both silly and vulgar, "not that the lady should wear handsome jewels, but that she should derive pleasure from the advertising." A reviewer at the 1906 National Academy of Design show responded in a very similar way to the overwhelming square footage devoted to some sixty portraits, most of which struck him (or her) as meretricious and false, because the painters had given in to the demand for the "prettiness and so-called *spirituelle*" that were the order of the day. It was unimaginable that a portrait painter, under such conditions, would attempt a "thorough" portrait. For all that, continued the reviewer, "The conscience is appeased when [the painters] give a customer his money's worth of mechanism, and, if at all cynical, they must laugh in their sleeves when taking the check to deposit. 'Stop, take notice,' say their canvases; 'I am the famous owner of this limned diamond tiara,' or else, 'I am the famous hostess or the valiant knight of industry,' and in contrast with this tumor of presumptuous loftiness the retiring, unaffected portrait has little show."[20] The portraits necessarily had to preserve a certain measure of decorum—they were hardly comparable in effect to the scandals or other intimate details insinuated in magazines like *Town Topics*. Nonetheless, in their very representation of individuals who may or may not have performed in official public posts, and who were just as often merely rich, stylish, or beautiful turn-of-the-century portraits collapsed private into public life, contributed to the cult of celebrity, which is now so entrenched a century later, and confirmed the all-pervading power of appearances.[21]

Appearances had everything to do not only with self-advertisement and self-aggrandizement at the turn of the century but also with a concerted and sometimes nearly desperate bid to affirm the natural genetic superiority of Anglo-Saxon bloodlines in the face of what threatened soon to become the sheer numerical superiority of eastern and southern European, Jewish and Catholic immigrants, who in the last third of the nineteenth century poured into America by the millions. The American press of the *fin de siècle*, haunted by the specter of degeneration on virtually every social front, helped fuel apprehension by printing innumerable articles and editorials decrying the evil times that had befallen the United States. Foreign mobs, bosses, and dictators seemingly undermined the vigor and integrity of the original Puritan stock, which, in one of those myths necessary to reality maintenance, was credited with all that was good, pure, strong—and now under siege—in America and its history.[22] Countering these fears, however, ran an alternative discourse, based on Darwin's theory of evolution as interpreted, moralized, and popularized by Herbert Spencer and certain American followers such as John Fiske. Spencer argued for a model of evolution based on a grand natural plan (as opposed to the virtually blind chance of natural selection model proposed by Darwin) for progress from lower to higher and material to spiritual. In concert with other sciences and pseudo-sciences, from anthropology to phrenology and physiognomy, the evolutionary model served as rationale to justify racism and social hierarchy by "proving" that the Anglo-Saxon type was the inevitable, intentionally designed product of that plan.[23] The most important signs of supremacy were inscribed in the physical characteristics of individuals, nationalities, and races. Faces, skull configuration, and coloring became part of a physical, readable text that furnished a guide to any person's place and importance on the scale of evolution from savagery to civilization.

The degree to which such indices of genetic and cultural status informed the population—the white middle and upper class portions of it, that is—can be gauged by the number of popular texts on physiognomy that enjoyed a healthy publishing history well into the twentieth century. Joseph Simms's *Physiognomy Illustrated*, for example, was brought out by Murray Hill in a tenth edition by 1891, and in 1913 M. O. Stanton's hefty *Encyclopedia of Face and Form Reading* (Philadelphia: F. A. Davis) originally published in 1889, was in its third edition. The racist taxonomies of such systems were predictably similar. The Simms book illustrated African- or Native-American faces (and occasionally Irish or Chinese) in contrast with those of white men as instances of underdevelopment of the qualities that spelled civilization. All the higher faculties were symbolized by refined, northern European or Anglo-American features. Even hair could tell a tale: fine, silky hair connoted cleanliness, while coarse hair betrayed filthy, swinish tendencies.[24]

Turn-of-the-century portraits, widely exhibited and often reproduced in illustrated magazines, performed the vital function of shoring up these crucial differences and proclaiming over and over again that the sitters—with their wealth, their acceptably British or Germanic or possibly French names, and their incontestably lofty status—were the highest evolved type in the world. The fact that because of educational and institutional barriers virtually no African-Americans, Native-Americans, or lower-caste foreigners emerged to exhibit portraits of individuals belonging to their own subcultures guaranteed that, at least within the walls of art academies, whiteness and approved bloodlines reigned supreme, while people of color appeared entertainingly in picturesque or exotic roles. By contrast, society portraits and even subject pictures based on portrait formats functioned implicitly as models not simply of ideal whiteness but as instructive examples of the best deportment and behavior. In most cases the painters themselves belonged to the same hegemonic company by virtue of ancestry and association.

This was especially true of Cecilia Beaux, all of whose sitters were, as Tara Tappert has characterized them, well-positioned, intelligent, upper-class Americans, most of them from Philadelphia, Boston, or New York.[25] As a member of a well-connected Philadelphia family of New England descent on her mother's side, Beaux had the advantage from the outset of being a social insider. Numerous commentators saw Beaux's own flawless social position as well as that of her subjects in her portraits. To one reviewer this position "explains the instinctive way in which she gives to her pictured subjects an air of natural ease and good breeding." To another she was virtually co-extensive with those she portrayed: "She is tall and slender, has gray eyes that look directly at one and are sometimes as luminous as her canvases . . . . She suggests the woman of highest breeding, of poise, of grace, or reserve . . . . It would be hard to imagine this elegant woman in velvet and rich furs claiming any of the license allowed to genius . . . . Her mother was a Puritan of New England, and gave her [a] conscience . . . ."[26] Beaux's *New England Woman* (Fig. 8) exemplifies the deep vein of Anglo-Saxon integrity that Beaux was able on occasion to mine. Not in this instance a representation of a society woman, the painting portrays Mrs. Jedediah Richards, an elderly cousin of the artist's grandfather, as a kind of whitewashed, impressionistic Whistler's mother who in contemporary eyes radiated the same aura as Whistler's mother, one of saintly maternity and selfless devotion. As Mrs. Arthur Bell put it, in *New England Woman*, Beaux had "gathered up with rare force and simplicity the whole story of a faithful and devoted life, into which no thought of self has entered to mar its usefulness." Faith, devotion, usefulness, purity: all of these attributes, of course, vividly evoked old New England, idealized in later times as a wellspring of American energies, virtues, and fortitude. This was a representative of a breed many feared might die out as alien hordes rushed in to trample out the past and overshadow the future.[27]

Sargent's *Mrs. Adrian Iselin* (Fig. 9) evokes a more contemporary sense of aristocracy and self-possession. As in Beaux's case, critics read into such portraits a merging of personalities; in Henry James's words, Sargent's subjects borrowed "something of nobleness from his brush," a sentiment later echoed by Charles Caffin when he wrote of Sargent's "instinctive refinement": "It would be quite impossible for him to have any feelings toward his subjects than those of a

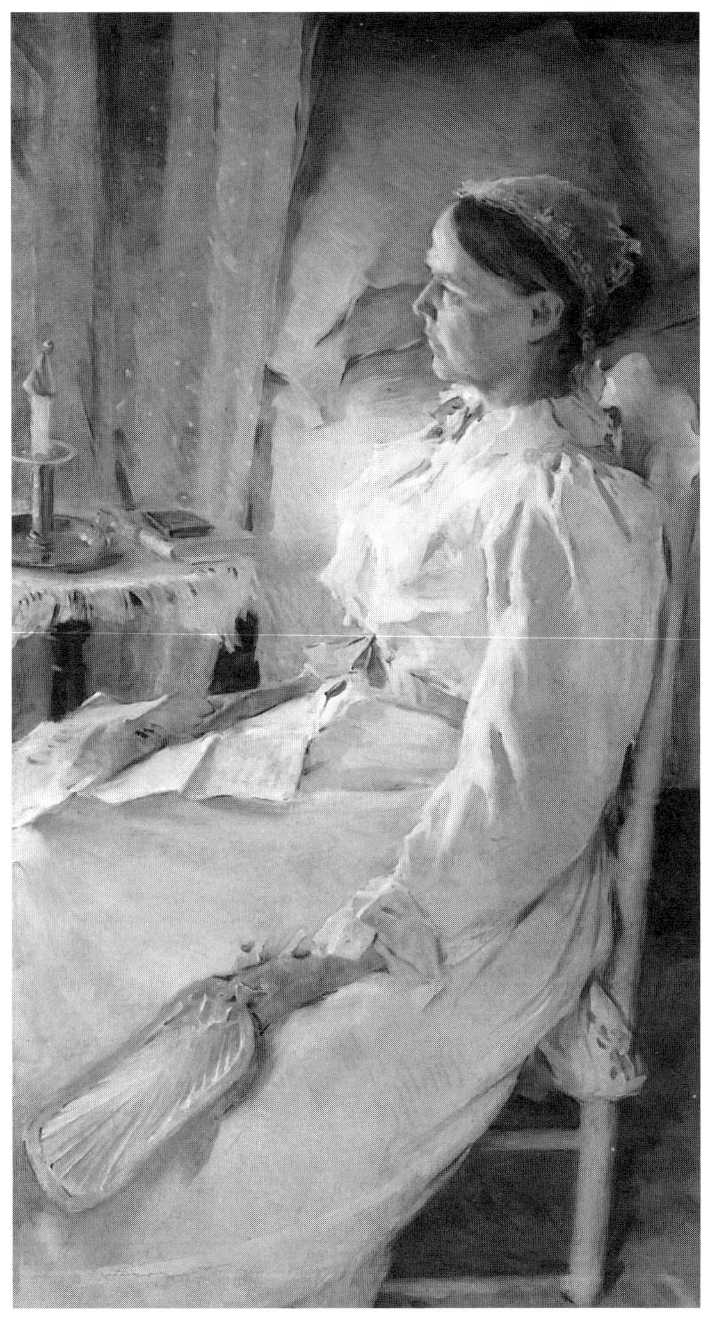

FIGURE 8 Cecilia Beaux, *New England Woman (Mrs. Jedediah H. Richards)*, 1895. Oil on canvas. The Pennsylvania Academy of the Fine Arts, Temple Fund Purchase.

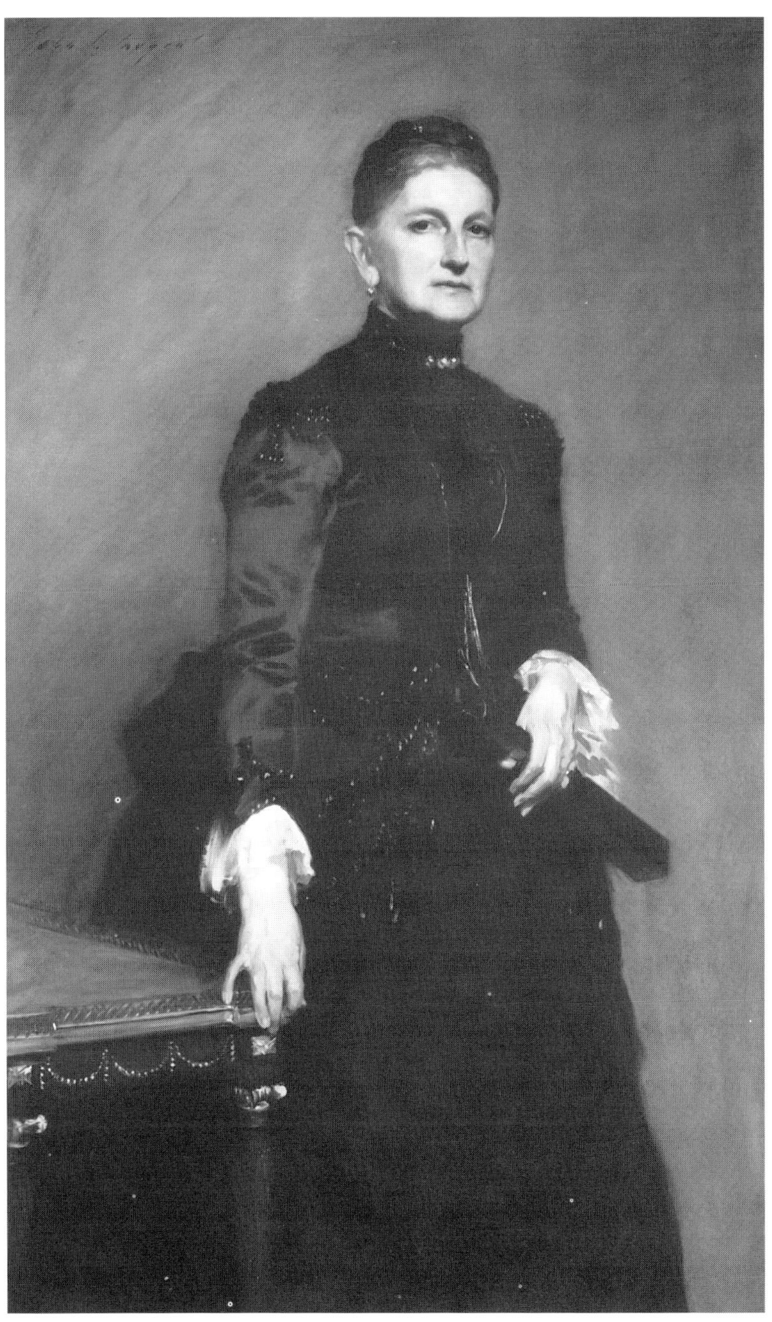

FIGURE 9 John Singer Sargent, *Mrs. Adrian Iselin*, 1888. Oil on canvas. National Gallery of Art, Smithsonian Institution, gift of Ernest Iselin.

true gentleman; and, though he may represent a lady in the full flavor of the modern spirit, he never allows the modernity to exceed the limits of good taste." Caffin's opinion here was sorely at odds with remarks he (and a number of others) had made elsewhere regarding Sargent's perceived callousness, yet that callousness too was a natural accompaniment to the painter's attitude of "unconcealed superiority" to his sitters.[28] Through his portraits Sargent proclaimed his own exalted aesthetic and Anglo-Saxon status while affirming, reinforcing, or at times even inventing the good breeding of his models. Both he and they stood forth as the finest fruit of progress in nature and civilization.

While the world of the society portrait remained a fairly exclusive one, the ideals of pure-blooded American aristocracy reached a much larger audience than exhibitions could ever accommodate through the illustrated weekly and monthly magazines of the 1890s and after. Most notable and notorious among a staggeringly vast new array of images was Charles Dana Gibson's "Gibson Girl" (Fig. 10), which first appeared in the pages of *Life* around 1890, and then in other publications, in special all-Gibson picture books, and in memorabilia of every kind. While this creature was a fiction, she promulgated, on a popular level, the same standards of breeding, superiority, and decorum as the portraits hanging in the National Academy of Design exhibitions; she functioned as a kind of lofty norm—a beacon for those who could aspire to her heights but equally an oppressive symbol of what many, doomed to be Other, could never attain. Harold Payne pinpointed the social function of the cartoons in observing that Gibson's work "savors of the drawing room, the club, or the boudoir. One is refreshed after seeing a series of his pictures, as he is by mingling with good society and hearing bright, crisp conversation." Percival Pollard, while gently chivvying Gibson for "growing" his Girl over the years to almost impossible heights, nonetheless relented: "Of what poise, what tact, what perfect balance she seems the embodiment! How well she hints at all that is finest, noblest, in the real, living flower, the American girl!" Pollard later reversed his position somewhat, or angled it anew, to deplore "undiscriminating young women" who vulgarized the Gibson Girl, and the debased ideal that had spread "in horrid profusion throughout the land." All of those real-life "girls" modeled on black-and-white pictures in magazines proved, said Pollard, "how essentially imitative is the average of taste in America; never was there a land so rich in beautiful women, and so poor in originality of adornment."[29] Pollard, however, did not quite understand the exact nature of relations between these would-be Gibson Girls and the original: it was as much a question of the immense power of images to shape consciousness as it was of willful imitation. While Pollard may have been disappointed at the degradation of the Gibson paragon by countless young admirers,

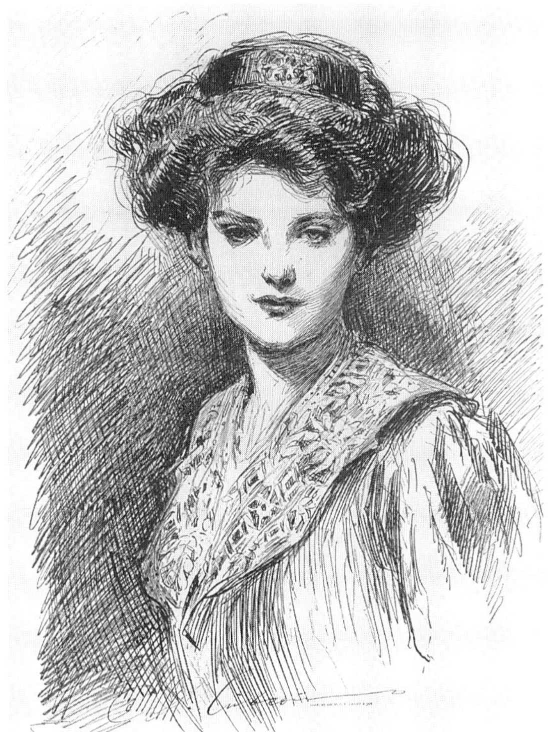

FIGURE 10 Charles Dana Gibson, *The Day Dream*, 1903. Photochemical reproduction of a pen-and-ink drawing. *Collier's* collection, Sarah Burns.

nothing could better demonstrate the authority that images were capable of wielding. Whether staring down from a wall or out from a page, images of wealth, elegance, and thoroughbred perfection set before the looking, reading public the finest phase of American evolution.[30]

A number of portraits and illustrations expressed or intimated the price, as well as the glory, of evolutionary progress. In this connection the dashing, sweeping style that animates their surfaces, along with compositional disequilibrium, function as visual encodings of what Americans and foreigners alike singled out as the cardinal, distinguishing American trait: electrical, restless, volatile, nervous energy. At the turn of the century, John Watson, an English traveler, registered his impressions of the American people. The American walk was not like the leisurely English pace; it was rapid, eager, anxious. Everything was approached in terms of speed. Americans would take an express elevator rather than a local one to save a mere minute's time; they were "mercurial" men "whose blood and whose brain[s]" were "ever on a stir." Even the climate was electric, the electricity having "passed into the people, who are simply vessels charged up to a certain number of volts."[31]

Sargent's striking double portrait of *Mr. and Mrs. I. N. Phelps Stokes* (Fig. 11), showing the two upper-class New Yorkers in their street clothes, successfully conveys a sense of high-strung quickness in the tall figure of Mrs. Phelps, with the emphatically temporary air of her jaunty pose; her almost awkward elbow; the broadly brushed planes of her skirt; and the small, neat head with tiny, super-refined features. While her not-quite-centered figure visually outweighs that of her husband, his presence in the shadowy background unbalances the composition sufficiently to enhance its casual, provisional air. Less dramatically, but tellingly, Sargent's *Mrs. Joshua Montgomery Sears* (Fig. 12) shows the interplay of tensions Sargent habitually incorporated into his poses: seated on the edge of a refined Louis XVI *fauteuil*, Mrs. Sears points her elbow into its back and supports the side of her face on two stiff fingers while her torso rotates in a counter movement accentuated by the arm she props on her thigh. Silvery fabric spills like rushing water down to the bottom edge of the canvas. While her face is calm, even shut, her body tells another story.[32] Many a critic thought that Sargent better than any other portrait painter had defined the quintessential spirit of the times. Royal Cortissoz responded to the force of Sargent's women, who illustrated "far more histrionically" than men "the nervous tension of the age." Christian Brinton's reactions were even stronger: faced with those "restless, vivid, spontaneous" images of modern men and women, he asked: "Is this neurosis or is it art? Perhaps it is both." It is true, of course, that Sargent's was an international style. Many of his English sitters looked as "nervous" as the Americans did. What is important for the discussion here is that critics claimed his stylistic peculiarities ratified the existence of a new, quintessentially American type.[33]

These critics might well have been reading into Sargent's portraits their own preoccupation with the phenomenon of modern nervousness, a topic of intense discussion and debate in the late nineteenth century, thought by some to be a distinctively American malady brought about by the breakneck speed of modernization. Dr. George M. Beard, who did much to diagnose and popularize the condition, described it as an affliction of the "indoor-living and brain-working classes" and attributed its epidemic spread to factors such as the advance of science, the telegraph, the periodical press, the speed of modern steam-powered transportation, and increased intellectual activity among women. By the 1890s many were calling nervousness America's national disease whose chief victims were "Anglo-Saxon Americans . . . especially those in the higher walks of life."[34] While there were no doubt many real sufferers, the sense of pervasive debility

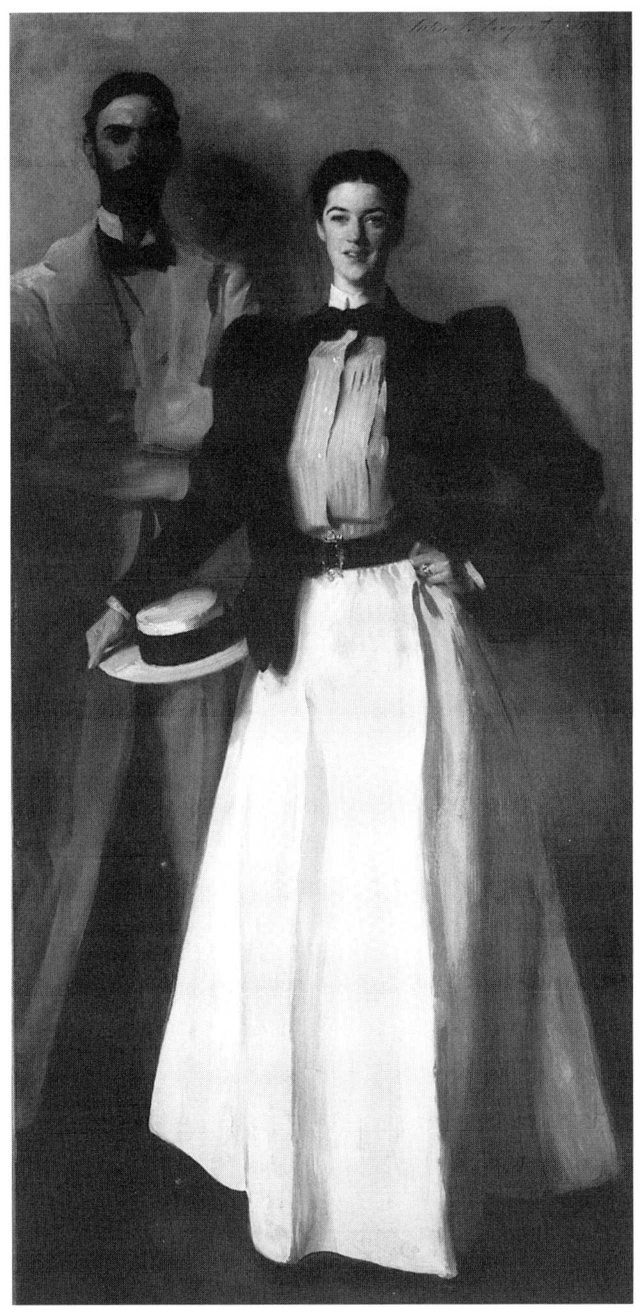

FIGURE 11 John Singer Sargent, *Mr. and Mrs. I. N. Phelps Stokes*, 1897.
Oil on canvas. The Metropolitan Museum of Art, bequest of
Edith Minturn Phelps Stokes, 1938.

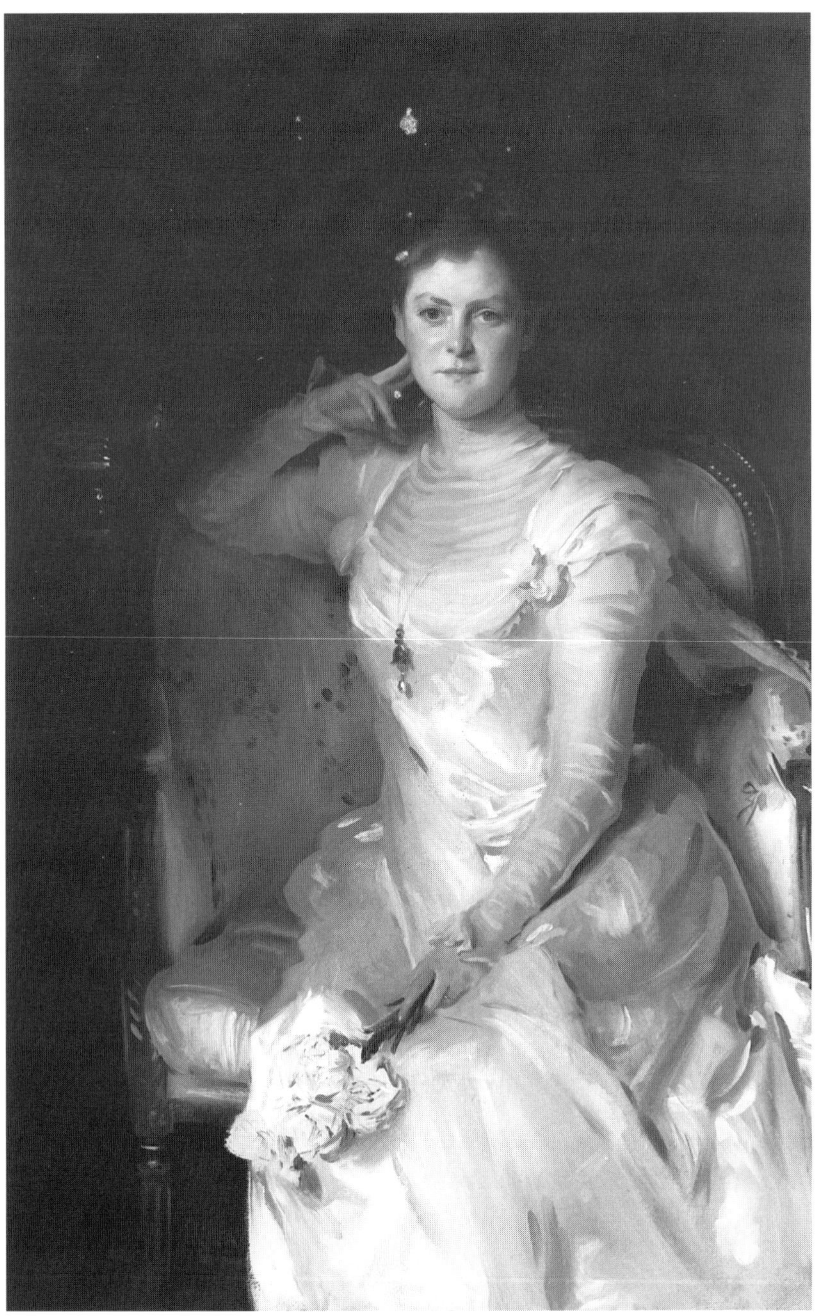

FIGURE 12 John Singer Sargent, *Portrait of Mrs. Joshua Montgomery Sears*, 1899. Oil on canvas. The Museum of Fine Arts, Houston, Museum purchase with funds provided by George R. Brown in honor of his wife Alice Pratt Brown.

and exhaustion, and the need to medicalize it, existed in part as social constructions arrayed against everything that rendered immigrant aliens both Other and dangerous: their supposed crude energies, their vigorous sexuality, and coarse sensibilities. Against such brute forces nervous Anglo-Americans might, on the one hand, seem terribly vulnerable; on the other, their supersensitivity betokened special status: "extraordinary intelligence and vivacity" were the natural complements of American nervousness and signs of the highest level of civilization ever achieved.[35]

Nonetheless, evolution had exacted a toll especially apparent in the modern woman. Classifying the "new American type," H. D. Sedgwick contrasted eighteenth-century English, French, and American portraits with those of Americans one hundred years later. Eighteenth-century portraits, he found, were all of a piece. They expressed what Sedgwick idealized as the prevailing eighteenth-century climate of social stability, mental calm, and solid values embedded in unquestioning acceptance of class distinctions, dogma, and belief. All of them portrayed "a pure national breed, wherein like bred with like in happy homogeneity." At the turn of the twentieth century, however, such purity was unattainable. Evolution had wrought inexorable change, producing a new, hybrid type, supremely flexible and adaptive, yet tormented by the birth pangs of the still unfolding evolutionary process. Women more than men bore the signs of this torment. Sedgwick viewed Sargent as the painter "born to depict . . . the strain of physiological and psychological transformation" and maladjustment. In portraits by John W. Alexander, (Fig. 13) he found another eloquent witness. How different were Alexander's women from those of Sir Joshua Reynolds, who happily blended "health and peace . . . grace and ease." Alexander's, by contrast, with their bizarre lighting and rippling, rhythmic lines, were anoretic lightening bolts. "Take a portrait by Mr. J. W. Alexander," wrote Sedgwick, "in which we see the indefinite, unphysical charm of American womanhood . . . . the restless pacing in the body's cage . . . . the American woman's body, too slight for a rich animal life, too frail for deep maternal feelings, seems a kind of temporary makeshift, as if life were a hasty and probably futile experiment."[36] Sedgwick's words, like the portraits he describes, also betray other sources of unease, stemming from the turmoil of the gender politics that few in the late nineteenth century could avoid. By seeming to extoll the experiment of evolution that had produced the still developing type of the American woman, Sedgwick masked and displaced the anxiety—widespread throughout middle-class American culture and entrenched in medical discourse—that women's increased demands and opportunities for education, legal rights, and worthwhile employment outside the home would impair their reproductive functions in addition to mitigat-

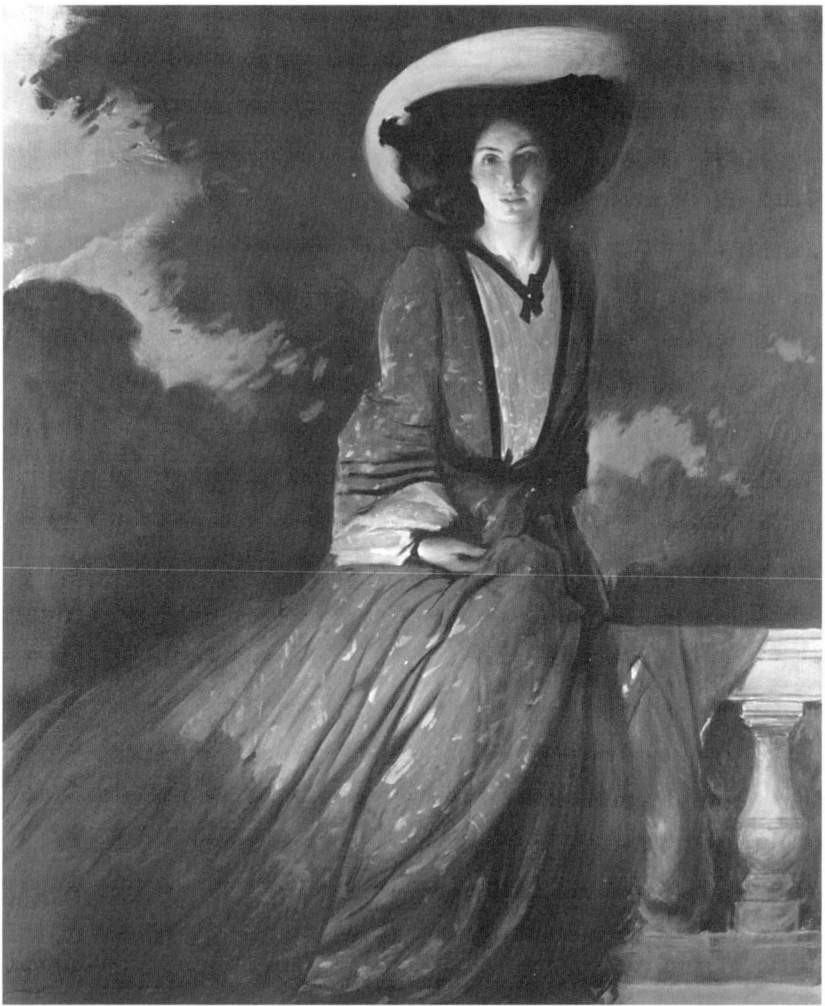

FIGURE 13 John White Alexander, *Portrait of Mrs. John White Alexander*, c. 1894. Oil on canvas. Los Angeles County Museum of Art, gift of Dr. and Mrs. Matthew Mickiewicz.

ing their subjection to men. This challenge to socially constructed gender roles threatened male and class hegemony alike and gave rise to every form of resistance, accommodation, and evasion. In Sargent's portrait the composition in which the aggressive, spotlit figure of Mrs. Stokes literally forces her husband into the background also hints at similar anxieties about the actual or feared ascendancy of feminine power.[37]

Both of these portraits stand as emblems of modernity and its discontents at the turn of the twentieth century. Each one is a complex melange of cosmopolitan flair, of decorative patterning, of tension and movement, of dramatic display, of intense expression, of refined development, taut nerves, and the murky politics of gender. The fluidity of Alexander's line, like the often hectic dynamism of Sargent's surfaces, might serve as metaphor for the all-pervading sense of change—and the anxiety and exhilaration it ushered in—that marked the lives of middle and upper-class Americans in the last decades of the nineteenth century. Whether highlighting good breeding, social worth, individual distinction, material luxury, or exquisitely sensitive nervous organization, turn-of-the-century American portraits maintained an often precarious balance between outward complacency and inner unease, the latter sometimes breaking through to hint at underlying disorders, broadly social as much as personal. Poised at the beginning of the twentieth century, the portraits of this era still have much to tell us, not only about their own time but about the roots of ours as well.

NOTES

1   William Howe Downes, "The Fine Arts," *Boston Evening Transcript*, January 2, 1892. On Sargent, see Carter Ratcliff, *John Singer Sargent* (New York: Abbeville, 1983).

2   Michael Quick, "Achieving the Nation's Imperial Destiny: 1870-1920," in Michael Quick, *American Portraiture in the Grand Manner: 1720-1920*, exhibition catalogue (Los Angeles County Museum of Art and National Gallery of Art, Washington D.C., 1981- 1982), 61-76, surveys the development of the quasi-impressionist style of society portraits during the late nineteenth century and after. On Beaux see *Cecilia Beaux: Portrait of an Artist*, exhibition catalogue (Pennsylvania Academy of the Fine Arts and Indianapolis Museum of Art, 1974-75); and Tara Tappert, "Choices: The Life and Career of Cecilia Beaux" (Ph.D. diss., George Washington University, 1990).

3   As noted by Frank Fowler, "Some Notes on Portraiture and the Recent Portrait Exhibition," *Scribner's Magazine*, 35 (March 1904): 380. According to Fowler, portrait exhibitions were of greater interest to the public than exhibitions featuring mixed subjects.

4   On the popularity of magazine portraiture and biography in the late nineteenth century see Theodore P. Greene, *America's Heroes: The Changing Models of Success in American Magazines* (New York: Oxford University Press, 1970), and Frank Luther Mott, *A History of American Magazines*, vol. 4: 1885-1905 (Cambridge: The Belknap Press of Harvard University Press, 1957), 152. "The Cost and Value of Sargents." *Literary Digest*, 45 (December 7, 1912): 1065 reported that Sargent was reputed to ask $5,000 for a full-length portrait, $3,750 for a half-length, and $2,500 for a head.

5 Richard Sennett, *The Fall of Public Man: On the Social Psychology of Capitalism* (1977; reprint. New York: Vintage Books, 1978), 21. For the impact of consumer culture on self-definition see T. J. Jackson Lears, "From Salvation to Self-Realization: Advertising and the Therapeutic Roots of Consumer Culture, 1880-1930," in Richard W. Fox and T. J. Jackson Lears, eds., *The Culture of Consumption: Critical Essays in American History 1880-1980* (New York: Pantheon Books, 1983), 3-38, and also Lears, "Beyond Veblen: Rethinking Consumer Culture in America," in Simon Bronner, ed., *Consuming Visions: Advertising and Display of Goods in America 1880-1920* (New York: W. W. Norton & Co. for The Henry Francis du Pont Winterthur Museum, 1989), 73-98. Warren Susman, *Culture as History: The Transformation of American Society in the Twentieth Century* (New York: Pantheon Books, 1984), 271-285, considers the transition from the autonomous self to the "other-directed" self in the early twentieth century.

6 Wilbur Larremore, "Anthropomania," *Atlantic Monthly*, 102 (November 1908): 668-669.

7 On Whistler's reaction to his portrait see Nicholas Pisano, *A Leading Spirit in American Art: William Merritt Chase, 1849-1916* (Seattle: Henry Art Gallery, University of Washington, 1983), 77-82.

8 Homer St. Gaudens, "Robert Henri," *The Critic*, 49 (August 1906): 131; Oscar Wilde, "The Decay of Lying," Edgar Saltus, introd., *The Writings of Oscar Wilde*, vol. 5 (New York: Gabriel Wells, 1925), 55.

9 *Life*, 16 (October 2, 1890): 175. The fact that the sitter has Irish features (as so often stereotyped in racist caricature of the time) adds irony to this representation, since only by looking like somebody else, i.e., not looking Irish, might this hapless individual escape prejudice in the nativist climate of late nineteenth-century America.

10 *Munsey's Magazine*, 20 (February 1899): 677.

11 *Ibid.*

12 William Crary Brownell, "American Pictures at the Salon," *Magazine of Art*, 6 (1883): 494; "Exhibition of the Society of American Artists," *Nation*, 38 (May 29, 1884): 474. For a detailed discussion of this portrait see Karal Ann Marling, "Portrait of the Artist as a Young Woman: Miss Dora Wheeler," *Bulletin of the Cleveland Museum of Art*, 65 (February 1978): 46-57. Kenyon Cox described Chase as a "camera" in "William Merritt Chase, Painter," *Harper's New Monthly Magazine*, 78 (March 1889): 549.

13 "The Fine Arts. The William Merritt Chase Exhibition," *Critic*, 7 (March 5, 1887): 115.

14 Quoted in Quick, "Achieving America's Imperial Destiny," 72.

15 Quoted in William M. Curtin, ed. *The World and the Parish: Willa Cather's Articles and Reviews*, vol. 2, 1893-1902 (Lincoln: University of Nebraska Press, 1970), 513.

16 Charles Caffin, *The Story of American Painting* (New York: Frederick A. Stokes Co., 1907), 257; Royal Cortissoz, "Books New and Old," *Atlantic Monthly*, 93 (March 1904): 413.

17 Trevor J. Fairbrother, "Painting in Boston, 1870-1930," in Fairbrother *et al.*, *The Bostonians: Painters of an Elegant Age, 1870-1930*, exhibition catalogue (Boston: Museum of Fine Arts, 1986), 66, and note 63, p. 90.

18 Henry James, "Charles S. Reinhart," *Harper's Weekly Magazine,* 34 (June 14, 1890): 471. See Richard Schickel, *Intimate Strangers: The Culture of Celebrity* (Garden City, New York: Doubleday, 1985).

19 [Richard Watson Gilder], "The Craze for Publicity," *Century Illustrated Magazine,* 51 (February 1896): 631-632.

20 "Fashion Notes," *Life,* 25 (January 10, 1895): 19; "The Gilder," "The Winter Exhibition of the National Academy of Design," clipping, 1906, Winslow Homer Papers, microfilm roll no. 2932, Archives of American Art, Washington, D. C.

21 See Stuart Ewen, *All Consuming Images: The Politics of Style in Contemporary Culture* (New York: Basic Books, 1988), on the modern culture of style, advertisement, and other forms of display.

22 See, for example, John H. Denison, "The Survival of the American Type," *Atlantic Monthly,* 75 (January 1895): 16-28, which compares modern America to the degenerate late Roman Empire, when the original Roman stock was gone. A canvass of any magazine with pretensions to seriousness around the turn of the century reveals an astonishing number of articles betraying fear of decay, upheaval, and change.

23 See Robert Bannister, *Social Darwinism: Science and Myth in Anglo-American Social Thought* (Philadelphia: Temple University Press, 1979). On the history and problems of racism and nativism see Ronald Takaki, *Iron Cages: Race and Culture in Nineteenth-Century America* (New York: Knopf, 1979) and John Bodnar, *The Transplanted: A History of Immigrants in America* (Bloomington: Indiana University Press, 1985).

24 Joseph Simms, *Physiognomy Illustrated; or, Nature's Revelations of Character* (1872; 10th ed. New York: Murray Hill, 1891), 224. On the use and misuse of these ideas see Joanne Finkelstein, *The Fashioned Self* (Philadelphia: Temple University Press, 1991), and Stephen Jay Gould, *The Mismeasure of Man* (New York: Norton, 1981).

25 Tappert, "Choices: The Life and Career of Cecilia Beaux," 437.

26 *Mail and Express,* cited in Clara Erskine Clement, *Women in the Fine Arts from the Seventh Century B. C. to the Twentieth Century A. D.* (1904; reprint. New York: Hacker, 1974), 38; Maud Carrell, "Pittsburgh Abreast of the Times in Art," *The Pittsburgh Dispatch,* April 9, 1911. Cecilia Beaux, *Background with Figures* (New York: Houghton Mifflin Co., 1930), 3-4, stressed the fact that her maternal grandparents were Puritans of English descent.

27 Mrs. Arthur Bell, "The Work of Cecilia Beaux," *International Studio,* 8 (October 1899): 220. The "alien hordes" language deployed here is not hyperbolic. Many a *fin-de-siècle* writer wrote of the ominous future in near-apocalyptic terms.

28 Henry James, "John Singer Sargent," *Harper's New Monthly Magazine,* 75 (October 1887): 691; Charles Caffin, *American Masters of Painting: Being a Brief Appreciation of Some American Painters* (New York, Doubleday, Page, 1902), 61-62; Caffin, "John Singer Sargent, the Greatest Contemporary Portrait Painter," *World's Work,* 7 (November 1903): 4100.

29 Harold Payne, "Our Caricaturists and Cartoonists," *Munsey's Magazine,* 10 (February 1894): 546; Percival Pollard, "Sundry 'American Girls' in Black-and-White," *Book Buyer,* 14 (June 1897): 475; Pollard, *Their Day in Court* (New York: The Neal Publish-

ing Co., 1909), 90. It is difficult to pinpoint the date when the first full-fledged Gibson Girl appeared. Gibson developed the type gradually, until it became distinctive enough to acquire its famous brand name.

30 Martha Banta, *Imaging American Women* (New York: Columbia University Press, 1987), 92-139 deals with some of the subjects I pursue here, but whereas Banta argues that the "type" of the new American Girl exemplified by Gibson's model was perceived as a worrisome hybrid, I believe that a strong argument exists for regarding it equally (in the eyes of the time) as a positive sign of advanced evolution. The fact that both positions enjoyed considerable currency is a sign of the deep ambivalence and uncertainty that marked social and cultural developments during this era.

31 John Watson, "The Restless Energy of the American People—an Impression," *North American Review*, 169 (October 1899): 568-574.

32 Albert Boime has described Sargent's use of contortion and strain as a response to the Aesthetic Movement's love of exaggerated posture and transformation of the body into a decorative object; see "Sargent in Paris and London: A Portrait of the Artist as Dorian Gray," in *John Singer Sargent*, exhibition catalogue (New York: Whitney Museum of American Art, 1986), 75-109.

33 Royal Cortissoz, "John Singer Sargent," *Scribner's Magazine*, 34 (November 1903): 529; Christian Brinton, "Sargent and His Art," *Munsey's Magazine*, 36 (December 1906): 281.

34 George M. Beard, *American Nervousness, Its Causes and Consequences* (New York: G. P. Putnam's Sons, 1881), 99; "Nervousness: The National Disease of America," *McClure's Magazine*, 2 (February 1894): 305. Studies of neurasthenia in the late nineteenth century include George Frederick Drinka, *The Birth of Neurosis: Myth, Malady, and the Victorians* (New York: Simon & Schuster, 1984), and Francis G. Gosling, *Before Freud: Neurasthenia and the American Medical Community, 1870-1910* (Urbana: University of Illinois Press, 1987).

35 Henry M. Lyman, "Nervous Disorders in America," *The Dial*, 2 (August 1881): 82.

36 H. D. Sedgwick, "The New American Type," *Atlantic Monthly*, 93 (April 1904): 538-540. See Mary Ann Goley, *John White Alexander (1856-1915)*, exhibition catalogue (National Collection of Fine Arts, Washington, D.C., 1976), and Sandra Leff, *John White Alexander 1856-1915: Fin de Siècle American*, exhibition catalogue (Graham Gallery, New York, 1980).

37 The background figure was originally to have been Mrs. Stoke's Great Dane, but the dog's refusal to pose led to its replacement by Mr. Stokes. On gender politics during this period, see Carol Smith-Rosenberg, *Disorderly Conduct: Visions of Gender in Victorian America* (New York: Knopf, 1985) and Michael S. Kimmel, "Men's Responses to Feminism at the Turn of the Century," *Gender & Society*, 1 (September 1987): 261-283.

Social Conflict and American Painting
in the Age of Darwin

KATHLEEN PYNE

———

THE LONG TRADITION of comparing American painters with the French Impressionists began in 1893, when the works of two Frenchmen—Claude Monet and Paul Bernard—and two Americans—John Twachtman and J. Alden Weir—were exhibited together at the same gallery in New York City. Critics assumed, because of the proximity of the works, that they should see some unity of purpose or style among the four. In actuality however, there was probably as little in common between Monet and the Americans as there was between Monet and Bernard, but no one seemed to question why these particular painters had been grouped together. Several reviewers concluded that the Americans had attempted to ape the French, thereby reading the relationship between the French and the Americans as a case of stereotypical American provincialism. Even as these critics assumed the Americans had taken the French as their models, they also expressed a great deal of surprise at how different the Americans were from Monet.[1] How curious it was that in paintings such as the *End of Winter* (Fig. 1), Twachtman seemed to have produced only pale, washed out versions of his Impressionist model.

These comparisons—one, that American painters in the 1890s were trying to do the same thing as French Impressionists, and two, that Americans failed to achieve the bold and radical vision of the French—have been recapitulated in histories of American art to this day. Some art historians have advanced the theory that American painters held back from adopting a pure, high Impressionist style because they wanted to preserve the integrity of the object instead of dissolving form into atmosphere, as Monet did. It has been reasoned that in the landscapes of Twachtman and his colleagues there still must have been some hold-over of the earlier belief that nature was sacred and therefore the integrity

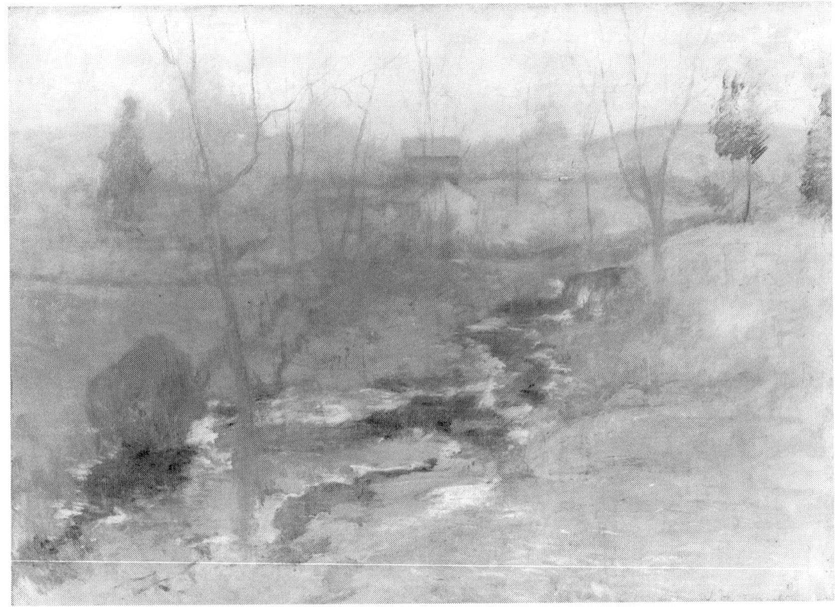

FIGURE 1 John Henry Twachtman, *End of Winter*, 1890-1902. Oil on canvas. National Museum of American Art, Smithsonian Institution, gift of William T. Evans.

of God's world had to be preserved.[2] In place of this theory, I would propose that Americans did fear dissolution, but that their reticence to adopt extreme fragmentation—the fear of dissolving form—was integrally related to pervasive concerns about the dissolution of the traditional social forms and philosophical truths that gave order and meaning to their lives.

When the frame of reference through which we view American Impressionism is shifted away from formal concerns to its social construction, the capacity of the term "Impressionism" to suggest what the paintings of Twachtman and his circle meant to their audience is diminished. That is, the landscapes and figure paintings of The Ten projected a very different world view from that explored by Monet. Scholars of French Impressionism, such as Richard Shiff, Joel Isaacson, Robert Herbert, T. J. Clark, and Linda Nochlin have made clear the importance of addressing the movement in terms of its implicit social and philosophical content, rather than viewing Impressionism merely as a stepping stone in the chain of events that led to twentieth-century abstract art. Within this larger social dimension French Impressionism carried within it assumptions that developed from positivism, a philosophy that preached a religion of humanity and a worship of empirical science rather than a transcendent realm.[3] Given this philosophical frame, a painting does not automatically qualify as Impressionist simply by virtue of its loose brushwork and bright color. To the contrary, broad brushwork and high-keyed color, as utilized by Twachtman, were read by his contemporaries to mean something quite opposed to a belief solely in the observable here and now. As will become apparent in this essay, the American understanding of French Impressionism in the 1890s arose from the particular social conditions Americans experienced at that historical moment in the northeastern United States. The work of the painters known as The Ten, including Twachtman, William Merritt Chase, Willard Metcalf, Childe Hassam, Weir, and others illustrates how crucial it is to consider the social and political dimensions of art, not simply the stylistic ones, when trying to determine the meaning of American art. To arrive at a good understanding of what American Impressionist paintings meant to the people who painted them and looked at them in galleries in the 1890s and the early twentieth century, it is essential to place that art into the context of the dilemmas and beliefs of the time, and not simply compare it to the art of the French or any other nation.

When we consider American Impressionism as a social construction, we must also answer questions relating to issues that concern the initial American resistance to this form of modernism: in other words, why is American Impressionism such a belated phenomenon; why is it taken up by the Americans 20 to 30 years after the French decade of Impressionism (the 1870s); and also why is American Impressionism so much tamer than the French version? Twachtman, for example, was a very savvy and well-educated artist who deliberately chose not to paint with the same degree of broken brushwork and jarring color juxtapositions that Monet and Renoir employed. He was trained in Paris and elsewhere on the continent, and he was, in fact, exposed to the Impressionist mode for more than a decade before he adopted the mannerisms of Impressionism in the early 1890s. If he were emulating the Impressionist idiom, then he deliberately transformed it into something tamer and quieter with a different purpose. His purpose, as he saw it, was to supply a sense of mental repose and harmony for the viewer, a therapeutic use of art that was as fitted to the needs of his peers as it was to his own private needs.[4]

The reasons that American painters like Twachtman first resisted the Impressionist idiom, and then modified it considerably, are illuminated by gaining some insight into the meanings the works of Monet and his colleagues held for educated middle-class Americans in the 1880s. In other words, before we can postulate why American painters modified French Impressionism, we have to know what it was they thought they were modifying. Therefore, we must first examine the American response to the French, and then turn to the American critique of the French evident in the works produced by The Ten during the 1890s and the first decade of the twentieth century.

Americans received their first extensive exposure to French Impressionism in 1886, when Durand-Ruel, the Impressionists' dealer who was in serious need of funds, went looking for another market for their works, and mounted an exhibition of almost 300 French paintings in New York City. Monet had been against this plan to send his pictures to the United States. "In Paris alone there is taste," he said, and there was no use attempting to seek it out in "the land of the Yankees." Of the pictures shown, about 250 were by the French Impressionists and their associates. The remaining fifty were by artists with whom Monet and Degas definitely would not have wished to be associated. The first gallery the visitor saw was very shrewdly installed, primarily with the works of these other painters. Here and there, a Manet or a Pissarro was slid between such conventional gallery fare as pictures of bulldogs, hunting dogs, horses, the village blacksmith, an organ grinder, exotic African scenes, and so on. Thus, the initial encounter with Impressionism was softened, and the viewer was gradually introduced to the shock of the bright blues and reds. But essentially, this strategy was to no avail. Monet was correct; there was little "taste" here as yet for the Impressionists. The show achieved the status of a sensation—a kind of *succès de scandale*, and few Impressionist works were sold.[5]

By no means did Americans respond uniformly to the new painting, but certain complaints appeared repeatedly in the reviews of the exhibition. This pattern of objections reveals something about the cultural climate that helped to shape American Impressionism. Individually, critics encouraged and discouraged artists in certain tendencies. But critics also expressed the cultural values shared by special groups at given points in time, and in this way their opinions can be understood to give voice to the pressures and the strains that permeate society at large. The pronouncements of critics who did not approve of Impressionism are fundamental to probing the Americans' objections to the French. In particular, the objections they made to the figural paintings of Manet, Renoir, and Degas pinpoint the type of Impressionist subject which profoundly disturbed viewers on these shores.

Just a few years before the big 1886 exhibition, Manet's *Woman with a Parrot* and the *Boy with a Sword* had been shown in New York. Termed "a scrawny old maid with a parrot" and "a disreputable dirty-looking boy," they were both held up as examples of "concentrated ugliness" mesmerizing in their "repulsiveness."[6] Manet's *Dead Christ*, which was meant to be an iconoclastic image, was also found to be "revolting" and materialistic.[7] Among Manet's works displayed in 1886 were his *Absinthe Drinker* and *Beggar Philosopher*, two

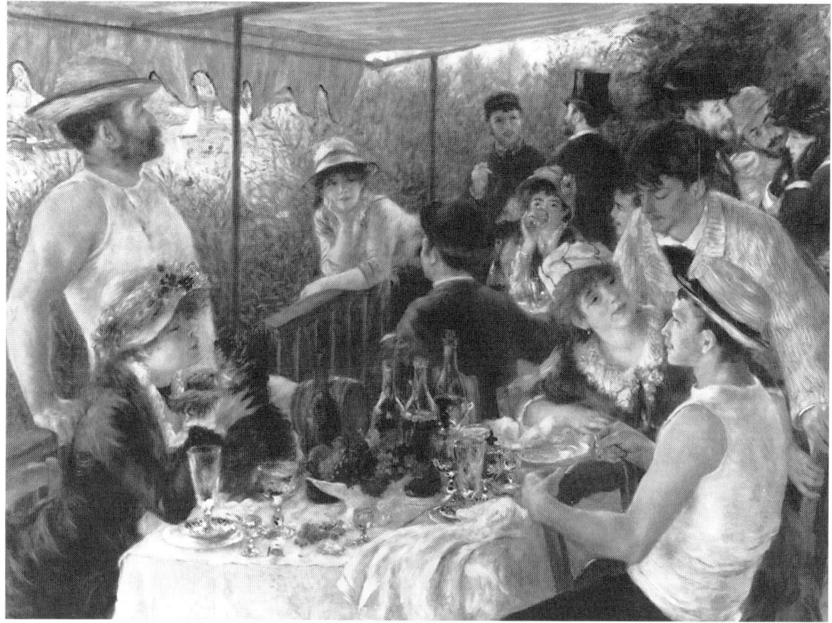

FIGURE 2 Pierre Auguste Renoir, *The Luncheon of the Boating Party*, 1881.
Oil on canvas. The Phillips Collection.

images of homeless men who had probably been displaced by the recent modernization of Paris. They led another writer to characterize Manet as a painter of "the most dyspeptic and suicidal manner conceivable."[8]

Degas was the French Impressionist whom Americans singled out as the most redeemable of the lot because he was so interested in aestheticizing lower-class subjects—café singers, laundresses and ballet girls—in weird, abrupt, but fascinating ways.[9] There were strident objections made to Renoir's *Luncheon of the Boating Party at Bougival* (Fig. 2) because its "vulgarity of color and types [which were] well nigh bottomless."[10] Renoir and Degas were both accused of glorifying coarse types and lower-class vulgarity. The persons depicted were selected from his own circle of friends, as well as patrons and collectors.[11] It is important to note that the assembled group was received as a depiction of the working class. Another of the French Impressionists, Gustave Caillebotte, exhibited an obvious image of working men in his *Floorscrapers*, in addition to several pictures of canoers on the river.

This small but representative sampling of criticism aimed at Manet and the French Impressionists brings the issue of class into focus as one of the elements in these paintings that was extremely unsettling to Americans. A writer for *Lip-*

pincott's Magazine succinctly explained this point. Criticizing the French Impressionists' vision of modern life, he said that they claimed to have evolved from the more idyllic vision of Barbizon painters. But in reality they reveled in the darkness of the urban corners frequented by prostitutes:

> . . .They immure themselves within the town-walls to paint studio, dramshop or theatre interiors, seeking freshness in the worn, painted, spectral faces such as haunt Baudelaire's verses, and gathering what Baudelaire has called the *fleurs de bitume.* If they go to the country at all, it is on a Sunday excursion just outside the city—to Asnières, Chatou or Bougival, where Paris has discharged her crowd of grisettes, with their attendant dry-goods clerks got up for the day as *canotiers* to make the river hideous with their loudness.[12]

The writer's contempt for the working class—the *grisettes* and dry goods clerks, as well as their lower-class social manners—is not at all disguised, nor is the disgust that such types would be given the privileged space of the painted canvas, a space traditionally devoted to the representation of the morally elevating subject.

This American discomfort with the working class as the subject of art surfaces in the art of The Ten, but only by its absence. When Twachtman's colleagues William Merritt Chase and Childe Hassam chose to paint the modern life of the city, they turned their sights to Central Park and Washington Square, in other words, areas that were the domains of upper-middle-class Anglo-Americans like themselves. They never depicted the newest social element in the city—the tens of thousands of immigrants who were pouring into New York through Ellis Island and taking up residence in squalid tenements in lower Manhattan, where roughly one half of the population of New York was crammed into 39,000 tenement houses during this period. The painters of The Ten simply averted their gaze from the urban underprivileged or edited them out of the cityscape. Thus, the socially-conscious vision was left to journalists like Jacob Riis, whose photographs of immigrants in their Manhattan slums were intended to rouse the middle class to action. It was only with the next generation, in particular the circle of Robert Henri, that American painters turned their attention to the underprivileged in America, although even the sympathetic rhetoric of this movement was not without a certain measure of the condescension and voyeurism inherent in the tourist's view of a foreign landscape.

An examination of the social tensions in the Northeast during the last quarter of the nineteenth century suggests that the hostility directed by the upper classes toward the lower-class subjects of the Impressionists signifies more than just the snobbery, or the ignorance and provincialism, of the art-buying American public. Though these social tensions have often been overlooked in recent art historical reviews of the 1880s and 1890s, this was a period in American history that was immensely troubled in every aspect of life. However, the reality of its turbulence has been exchanged for a view of the period as the "Gay 90s" or the Gilded Age. Even though it was considered a carefree age concerned with the pursuit of pleasure and material wealth, there were many at the time, such as the philosopher Charles Pierce, who saw it more vividly as an "Age of Pain."[13] For the Anglo-American upper classes the changes they were forced to confront produced more anxiety than excitement, and their pain is made more evident by revisiting the series of economic downturns and social displacements, as well as philosophical and religious crises that began directly after the Civil War. After an entire generation of men had been lost in the war, evolutionary science immediately seemed to assault traditional religious beliefs about the structure of the universe.[14] The lack of certainty over the existence of God or about life after death made the sacrifices of the war especially hard to bear. And then, with the advent of an incoming "foreign" population of non-Anglo-Saxon Protestants in the 1880s, the whole structure of American society began to shift.

At the same time the workplace was transformed from a small shop to a large impersonal corporation, and industry was annually plagued by chaos. Each decade of the late nineteenth century experienced a major depression. Workers bore the greatest brunt of these economic downturns, and by 1889 eighty-five percent of all industrial workers lived below or just above the poverty line of five hundred dollars a year. Not that they submitted to such low pay and long hours passively. Nearly 10,000 strikes shook the American workplace over the ten-year period from 1880-89. In 1886 alone, the year called the Great Upheaval, almost 700,000 workers went on strike, and many of these strikes were violent. Workers, perceived as primarily foreign (although only one-third of all industrial workers were immigrants) and blamed for this unrest, were thus condemned as anarchists.[15] Political cartoons such as "The Evils of Unrestricted Immigration" (Fig. 3), which shows a swarm of hardened-looking immigrants coming off the boat at Ellis Island with hats labeling them as German socialists and Russian anarchists, plainly spoke to these fears.

While visualization of such tensions was common enough in the medium of illustration, the sole representative in the medium of painting that recorded or commemorated this kind of conflict is *The Strike* (Fig. 4) by Robert Koehler, a painting which was shown at the National Academy in 1886. Not only was 1886 the year of the great New York Impressionist exhibition, but it also saw the most violent and the greatest number of labor uprisings of any year in this period. Shortly after May Day, protest culminated in the Haymarket Riot in Chicago in

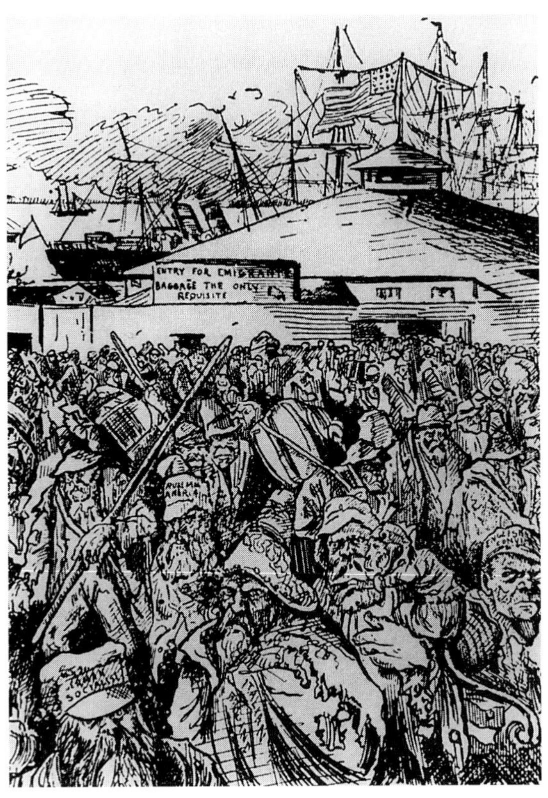

FIGURE 3 Hamilton, *The Evils of Unrestricted Immigration*, 1891. Cartoon. From *Judge*, March 28, 1891.

FIGURE 4 Robert Koehler, *The Strike*, 1886. Oil on canvas. Deutsches Historisches Museum, Berlin.

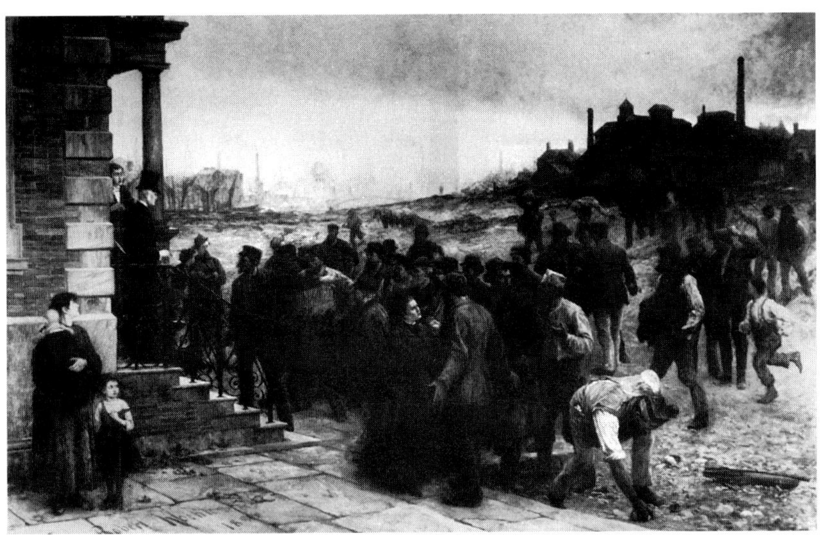

which one policeman was killed, seventy policemen were injured by a bomb thrown into the police line, four demonstrators were shot, and seven anarchists executed afterward for a crime in which there was no evidence of their complicity.[16] After this picture Koehler never again depicted a political subject, and the painters who later exhibited together as The Ten never approached this subject matter. It is interesting that Koehler was born in Germany, and his family immigrated to the Midwest where his father worked as a machinist. In comparison, most of The Ten could trace their ancestry back to the seventeenth-century English men and women who were among the first settlers in the Northeast; obviously, they had much invested in the status quo.[17]

The politics of change in America presented a telling contrast to the politics of change in France: at the same time that the urban redesign of modern Paris was so exciting for the Impressionists (who, according to T. J. Clark, represented the bourgeois position of the Second Empire[18]), social transformation in the American arena was not regarded as unconditionally consonant with progress. Unless it was of the prescribed evolutionary order, meaning slow, gradual modifications and refinements of Anglo-American cultural norms, it could be interpreted as producing physical mutation and moral perversity.

Against this background of anxiety, this climate that seemed to portend an impending social Armageddon, it is hardly surprising that the art-buying upper-class public did not want to see the great unwashed and unenlightened, whom they suspected were potential bomb-throwers, celebrated in the canvases of contemporary painters. Just as the Union was recovering its lost unity, the country again seemed to be on the verge of cataclysm, but this time in a war of classes. It was feared that the more robust peasant races (in other words, Catholic and Jewish peoples from the south and east of Europe) would be pitted against the Anglo-Saxon race (the founders of the country) whom it was thought had grown weaker and more genteel in settling comfortably into the Northeastern part of the United States.[19]

In view of this threat of chaos, the Darwinian "struggle for survival" was never out of mind for long. In fact, Darwinism, both as a metaphor and as a scientific theory, framed the social conflict, and predictably, friction between classes was understood in those terms.[20] But what is perhaps more revealing of the nature of the American resistance to French Impressionism is the way in which the dreaded specter of Darwinian struggle, particularly of a class war, could be intimated in an artistic mode, especially a method based on violent contrast or barbaric color, as the landscape style of Monet and Renoir was perceived to be. Several American critics straightforwardly accused the French Impressionists of harboring sentiments of the "radical and the rioter."[21] Viewed within the Darwinian paradigm, the technique of the French implicitly advo-cated political and social extremes. It was said that Manet, for example, showed "nature out of tune" and that Renoir's colors "shrieked."[22] Monet's use of com-plementary colors and his broken brushwork seemed unnecessarily aggressive and violent, and the French Impressionists were seen as spreading chaos and ri-oting in the wake of their exhibitions.[23] While a handful of collectors purchas-ing pictures by Monet in the years following the Durand-Ruel exhibition were either newly rich industrialists who admired Monet's "scientific" and honest vision or speculators in the art market who hoped to cash in on the latest form of cultural capital, the much larger number of Americans collecting the Barbi-zon school were by and large establishment types who preferred to invest in Corot's and Rousseau's quiet tonalities for their nostalgic gloss on the har-monies of the rural past.[24] In fact, as late as the Armory Show in 1913, Darwinian thought still conditioned Americans to think of art that was violent in its frac-turing of form or primitive and barbaric in its expressionistic color as regres-sion, a giant leap backward against the general progress of human civilization.[25]

This sense of civilization—in contrast to the perceived savagery of French Impressionism—is precisely what the paintings of The Ten held out to viewers in the 1890s. Theirs is basically a tonal mode that has only general affinities to French Impressionism in the breadth of its brushwork and high-keyed colors. Based on tonal harmonies, American Impressionism constituted a vision that offered reassurances to the most pressing questions of the day, unlike the art of Monet. In the face of Darwinian struggle in nature and the struggle in human society, it seemed that all harmony of the individual with the world had been lost. What was wanted at that time in works of art was a reassurance that har-mony and unity could be recovered for both the individual and the community.

When we consider the ways in which American painters adapted Impression-ism to the American scene, we find that images of the city and the countryside come into view as the two major categories within which they worked, while subsidiary categories might be designated as scenes of middle class leisure—at the beach, for example—and figures in interiors. Some allusion has already been made here to the highly selective vision of Hassam and Chase as they sur-veyed the metropolis of New York; a closer examination of their strategies is now in order. In approaching the metropolis of New York in the 1890s, Childe Hassam constructed an urban environment that defined the progress of Ameri-can civilization. Hassam focused on what was then considered uptown, the bur-geoning commercial and theatre district that stretched along Fifth Avenue from Washington Square to Union and Madison Squares (fig. 5). Manhattan in this period was considered the most dangerous of American cities because, with the

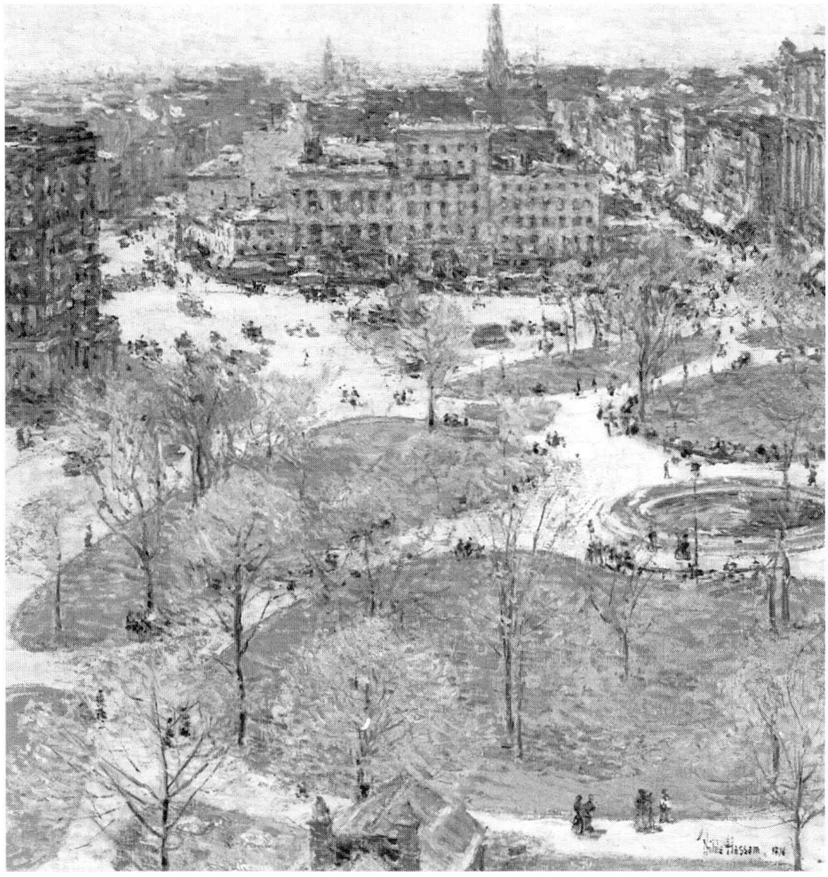

FIGURE 5 Frederick Childe Hassam, *Union Square in Spring*, 1896. Oil on canvas. Smith College Museum of Art purchase.

tens of thousands of foreigners crammed into warren-like tenements at the southern tip of the island and new millionaires relocating in sprawling mansions uptown, relations between classes were volatile. A sense of discontent among the lower classes and of hysteria in the urban elite over the danger they presented led to despairing assessments of American society, and particularly to a characterization of the city as the breeding ground of criminals and anarchists.[26]

Hassam countered the idea of the city as a social menace, however, by presenting the avenues of New York in a grand panoramic sweep of space filled with glittering white neoclassical hotels and office buildings that are connected by streets arranged in a radial pattern. Hassam had learned this strategy, which spoke of civil order and regulation, from his experience with the broad, tree-lined boulevards of Paris a few years earlier.[27] In some of his earlier pictures, he came close to the vision of the French Impressionist Gustave Caillebotte, but significantly, he replaced Caillebotte's critique of the mechanical and monotonous quality of the designed urban environment with a domestic narrative that offers a more optimistic view of the city.[28] By integrating the buildings of midtown with the treetops of the park, Hassam's ordered prospects of New York, dating from the early 1890s, suggest that nature and culture are in perfect harmony here. Though these scenes are viewed from the bird's-eye perspective, enough detail has also been given to the costumes of the small figures to identify the prospect as the glamorous milieu of the upwardly mobile. When the perspective is that of the street level, even if a street sweeper might be caught within the frame, the threat of potential social discord is mitigated by the institutionalized uniform he wears, as well as his distance from the more genteel strollers in the picture.[29]

Inside Manhattan's parks in the works of William Merritt Chase, the environment is light and airy, not unlike that of Hassam's New York. The feeling of wide, open space Chase created in these scenes (Fig. 6) was influenced both by direct observation and by the Japanese prints Chase collected. In Chase's paintings the greenswards are evoked as refuges from the struggle of the streets, places where the individual can still experience a sense of solitude in a therapeutic moment before going back into the noise and the crush of the crowd that waited just outside these quiet enclosures. Central Park was intended by its designer, Frederick Law Olmstead, to function as a democratic preserve where different classes would meet and the lower classes improve themselves by learning from the upper. In the late nineteenth century, however, the park was as yet largely the province of the upper classes, and Chase pictured it accordingly, populated by well-dressed children, sometimes escorted by their nannies.[30]

At other moments in representing the topography of Manhattan as a landscape of progress, Hassam and Weir (Fig. 7) utilized the tonal strategies of Whistler's atmospheric veils: the delicate beauties of the snow or the deep nocturnal blues in which small glittering lights represent human presences are invoked to suggest a political concordance, that the city too could be a site of social harmony.

In interpreting the countryside, the generation of the 1890s adopted an imagery that might be termed that of a filiopietistic landscape. In other words, the Ten revered the landscape of their forefathers as they paid homage to what they feared was a vanishing Anglo-American heritage. This affectionate gesture was achieved essentially through a nostalgic process of cataloguing the pre-indus-

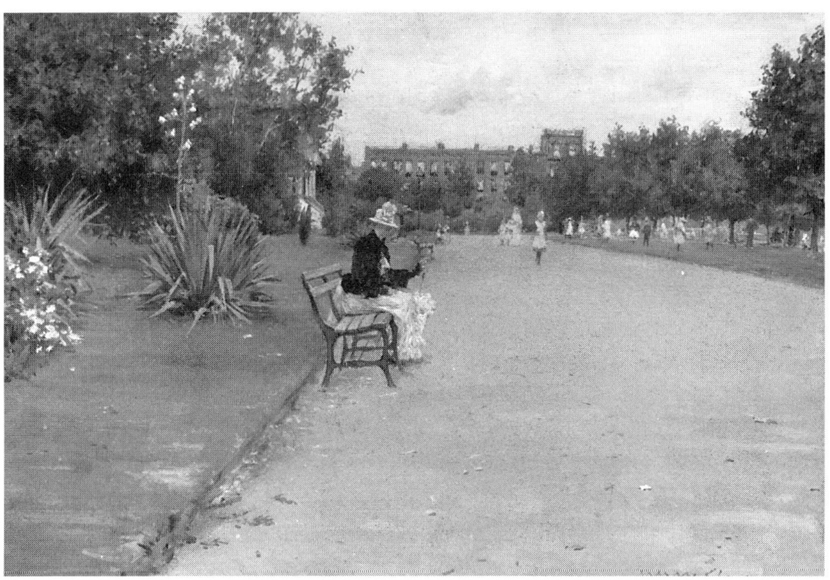

FIGURE 6 William Merritt Chase, *The Park*, c. 1888. Oil on canvas.
The Art Institute of Chicago, bequest of Dr. John J. Ireland.

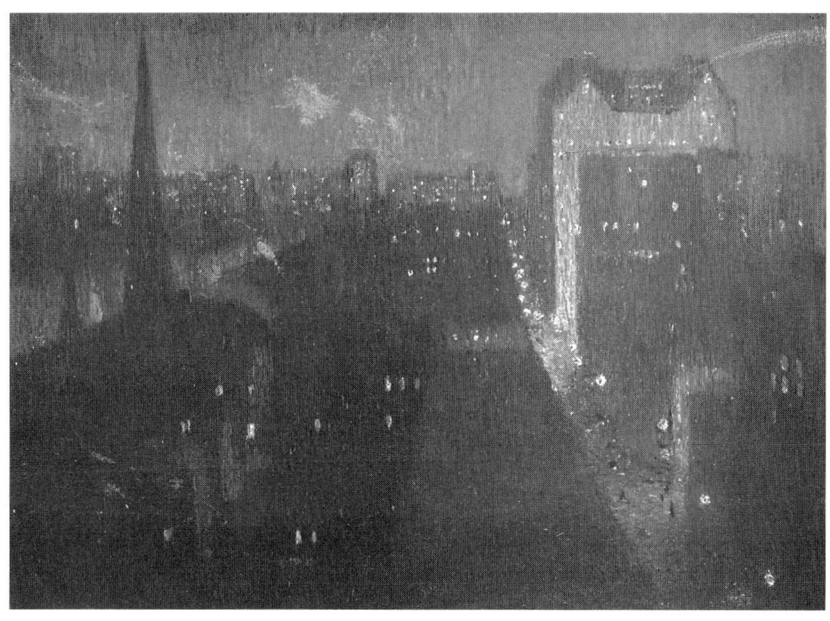

FIGURE 7 Julian Alden Wier, *The Plaza: Nocturne*, 1911. Oil on canvas.
Hirshorn Museum and Sculpture Garden, Smithsonian Institution,
gift of Joseph H. Hirshorn, 1966.

trial character of the New England town. Both Metcalf and Hassam were masters of this type of landscape. Metcalf's panoramic views of Massachusetts and Vermont towns (Fig. 8) typically are filled with churches and meeting houses with white neoclassical porticos, country stores, tree-lined avenues, ancient town oaks, and quaint figures in country attire. A large number of Hassam's and Metcalf's works in this category depict preindustrial occupations such as agriculture, the village blacksmith, and boat building, before factory production had gained the edge in the economy of the region. With industrialization, foreign workers attracted by jobs flooded into the area, and the demographics changed radically. By the 1890s New England had lost its traditional Anglo-Saxon Protestant homogeneity.[31] Hassam's and Metcalf's contemporary images of New England scenery with their carefully selected landmarks might thus be read as a form of wishful thinking. Attempting to convince the viewer that these earlier conditions predominated at the beginning of the twentieth century, Hassam (Fig. 9), in particular, rehearsed the symbols and signposts that defined the nation as a product of its Anglo-Saxon past: colonial churches, historical eighteenth-century houses, charter oaks, and ancient elms located in the town square. By overlaying these hallowed symbols of Anglo-Saxon history with a gloss of dappled sunlight and freshly observed atmosphere, Hassam asserts with his pictures of New England that the past still lives in the present. This antiquarian trope sold so well that Hassam proliferated it in the medium of etching (Fig. 10) well into the 1920s, and it inaugurated what was to be the most profitable period for several members of The Ten in the first two decades after the turn of the century.[32]

New England filiopietism is but one aspect of the American resistance to the modern agenda of French Impressionism; it signals a resistance to the French embrace of the technological and industrial environment—a resistance that characterizes American painting as a whole in the 1890s. The late nineteenth-century viewer could be reassured that an earlier social order was intact by an art that acknowledged, and yet downplayed change. Such a strategy is evident in the rural imagery of J. Alden Weir. Though initially upset at the signs of modernity that were appearing around his home in Branchville, Connecticut in the 1890s, Weir took a different approach and attempted to show that iron bridges (Fig. 11) and white factories could be aesthetically pleasing and even integrated into the pastoral New England landscape to look "natural," as if they had always been there.

While the first American Impressionists lived for the most part in New York and Boston, most managed to spend a good deal of time in the New England countryside as well. Twachtman and Weir opted to live in Connecticut at a time

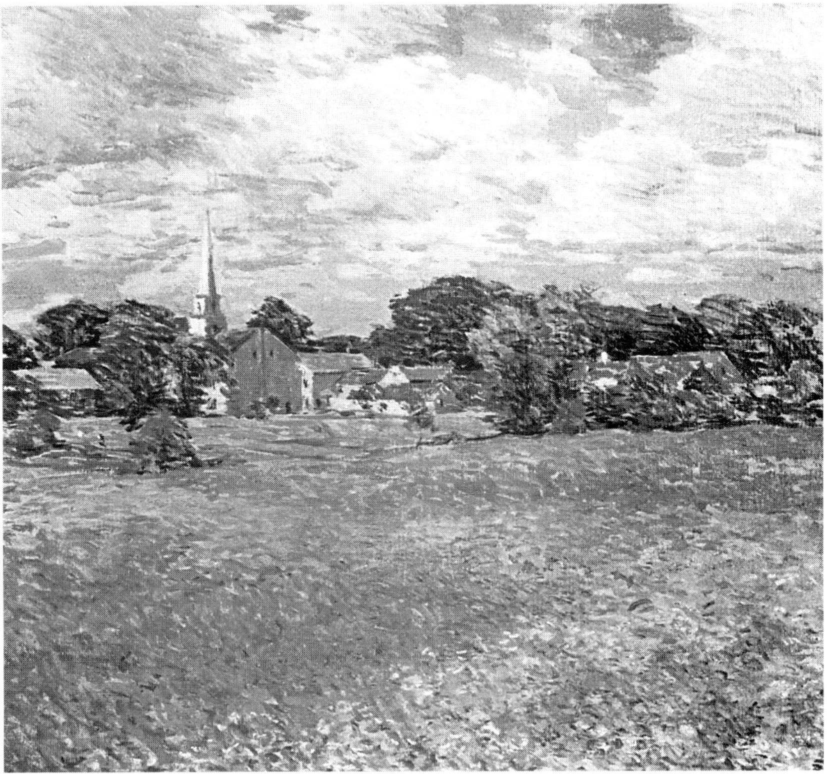

FIGURE 8 Willard Leroy Metcalf, *Buttercup Field*, 1920. Oil on canvas.
Telfair Academy of Arts and Sciences, Inc., Museum purchase.

when the train made commuting to work in the city and maintaining a home in
a garden suburb relatively convenient. On their Connecticut farms they focused
repeatedly on the Arcadian niche that, like the bit of nature in the city park,
promised the experience of silence and the recuperation of psychic equilibrium.
Twachtman's landscapes intimate that nature still responded to the psychic
needs of men and women—even after Darwin had to a great extent reframed
nature as the site of struggle and death, or in Tennyson's words, "red in tooth
and claw." Even so, Twachtman's winter landscapes spoke to his contemporaries
of spiritual regeneration during a season when life had seemingly disappeared
from the earth.

Something very different from French Impressionism was suggested by
Twachtman's art to patrons in 1893. He did not simply tone down Monet's vibrant color and smooth out the broken brushwork. Rather, he started from a

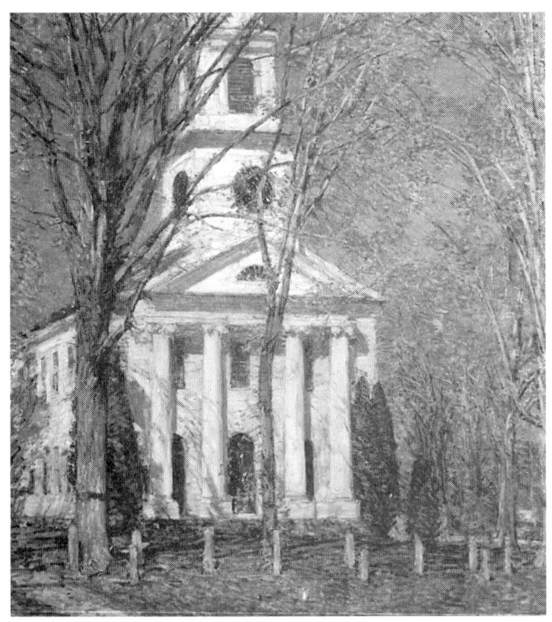

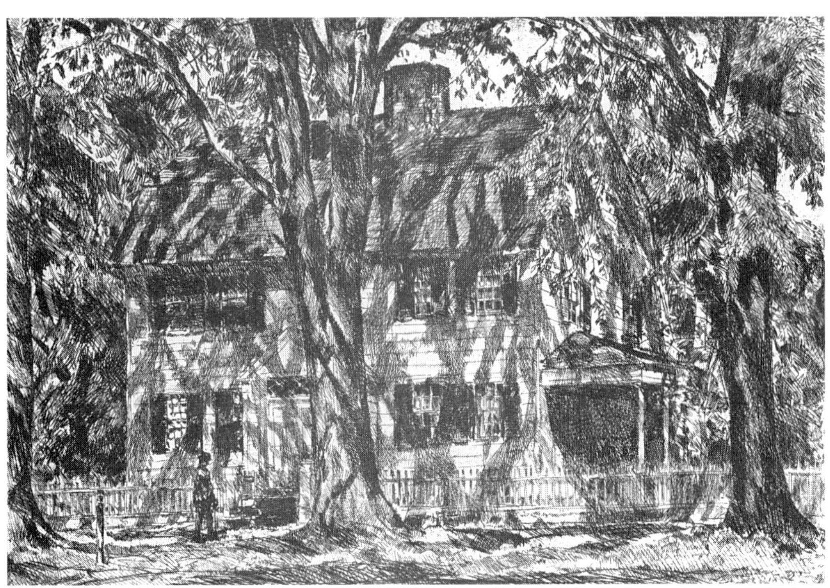

FIGURE 10 Frederick Childe Hassam, *The Lion Gardiner House, Easthampton,* 1920.
Etching on wove paper. Georgia Museum of Art, the University of Georgia,
university purchase. GMOA 79.3969

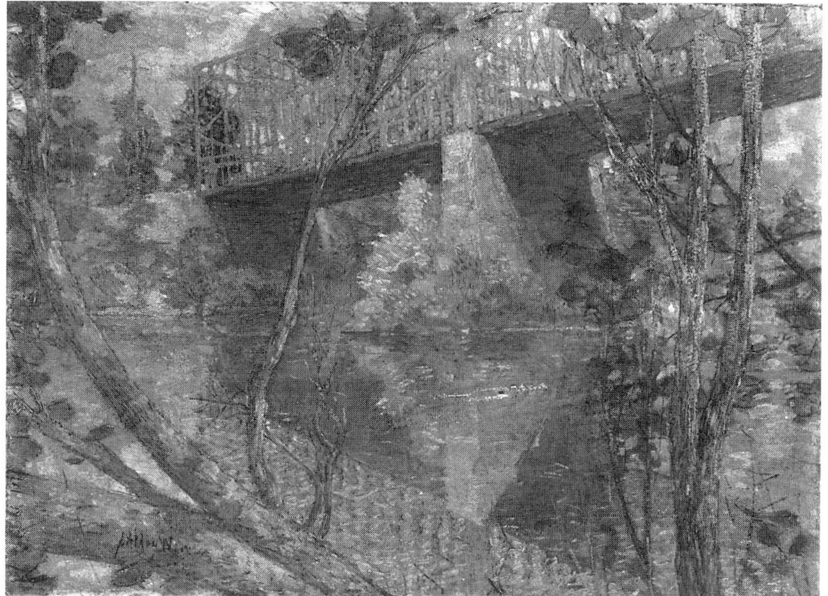

FIGURE 11 Julian Alden Wier, *The Red Bridge*. Oil on canvas. The Metropolitan Museum of Art, gift of Mrs. John A. Rutherford, 1914.

different point of view altogether—the view that valued the quality of repose, as expressed in tonal harmonies, as the highest purpose of art.[33] In paintings such as *Winter Silence* (Fig. 12), he tightly controlled the color and tone, reducing the number of shades to a few blues and mauves and salmons in a manner similar to Whistler's abstraction in the "nocturnes." This Whistlerian tendency to go toward the middle range of tone, or to add grey to the color, was rare in Monet's work during his high Impressionist period of the 1870s and 1880s, when he depended on a greater contrast of intensity and hue to produce the sparkle and vibrancy of light. Monet was frequently entranced by capturing the bright light of afternoon, while in the 1880s and early 1890s Twachtman was concerned with projecting a mood, usually melancholy, onto the landscape in the manner of Whistler's "nocturnes" through the use of cool, muted tones.

Close tonal harmonies are common to The Ten, especially Hassam and Weir. Their colors tend to cohere around the middle tones and hues that are similar, not complementary or opposite. They also added a good deal of white to their colors instead of using highly saturated hues, the jewel tones of pigments just squeezed out of the tube, because they were interested in color harmonies, not dissonances or abrupt shifts and contrasts. Even when they indulged in broken

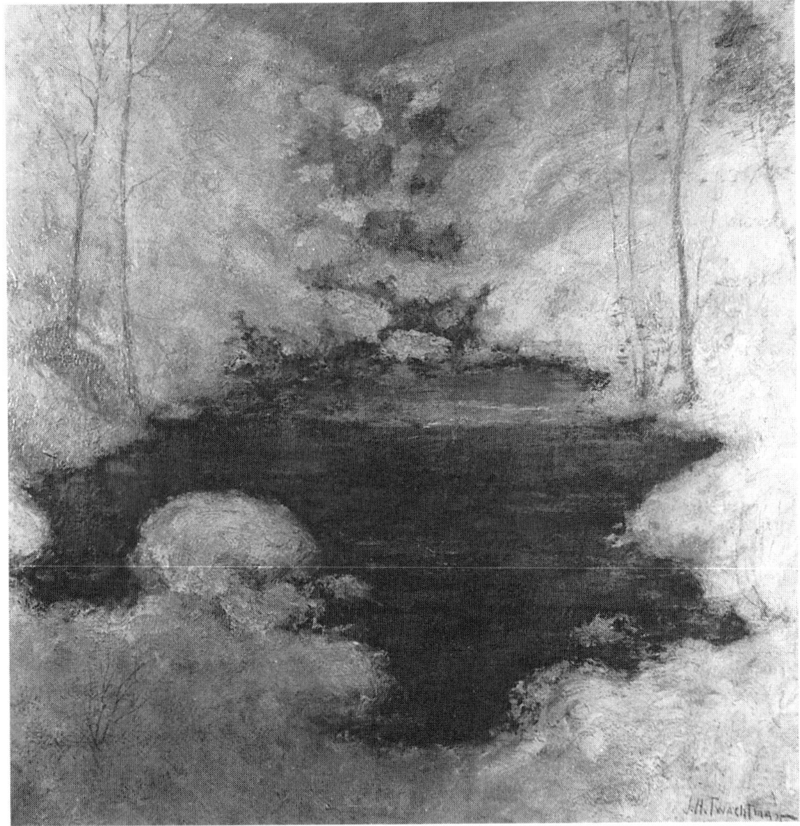

FIGURE 12 John Henry Twachtman, *Winter Silence*. Oil on canvas.
Mead Art Museum, Amherst College, gift of Clay Bartlett.

brushwork, for example Hassam's small glittering stroke, they fused Whistlerian harmony with this type of active application. In short, they quite often ameliorate the Impressionist system; they tone it down and make it quieter.

Quiet and comfort, Twachtman wrote to Weir in 1885, described the state of mind that the ideal painting should effect upon the viewer, and in his French paintings he was already working toward this mode.[34] At the end of the 1880s, living on his farm in Greenwich, Twachtman did a series of pastels that taught him how to achieve the muted and delicate color effects he desired in oil. Transferring the soft, de-materialized approach to form that he achieved in his pastels to his work in oil painting, Twachtman worked toward a mood that ministered to the human need for the tranquility and the solace of nature. In this way his intent approached a non-Western tradition of painting, namely that of the Sung Dynasty painters who in twelfth- and thirteenth-century China produced landscapes of great subtlety and delicacy. Though Twachtman may never have seen these paintings, he was quite probably familiar with the Japanese versions of them that flooded into the United States in the late nineteenth century, just as he was keenly interested in Japanese prints in the early 1890s. Moreover, Twachtman's study of Buddhist religious texts at that time would have offered him a philosophy that prized tranquility in the silence and flux of nature, a philosophy that was encoded in these Chinese and Japanese landscapes.[35] In fact, Twachtman used the property behind his house at Greenwich much as the Chinese sage used his garden, as a refuge from the world which so disappointed him. A lack of patronage and critical support for his work led Twachtman to turn to alcohol, while he also suffered from malaria and the death of two of his children in the 1890s. If Twachtman was a troubled man with something "gnawing at his soul," he depended on the seemingly feminine responsiveness and the profound quiet of nature for a kind of emotional therapy that would mitigate the harsh blows the world dealt him.[36]

Though Twachtman was from the Midwest, he—like Theodore Robinson— abandoned the flat, wide-open spaces and the ascetic vistas of Midwest farms for the intimacy of the rolling Connecticut hills. He seemed obsessively drawn to the brook on his property as a source for his work, and in his paintings of the brook and the pool, he tried to re-create his own experience there by forcing the viewer into the elliptical niche of space formed by the banks and the trees blanketed with snow. He located a structure in the landscape, the bowl of space carved out by the brook, that draws the viewer into the space so that there is a sense of being enfolded by the soft, cool textures of water and snow-covered earth. In their countless New England pastorals Weir and Metcalf (Fig. 13) followed this Arcadian-niche format as well. Here, nature is offered to the viewer as a nurturing place that can always be counted upon to answer the need many upper-class Anglo-Americans felt at this moment for tranquility and permanence in the face of overwhelming change.

Other Boston members of The Ten such as Tarbell and Benson made scenes of middle-class leisure in the garden- or home-setting the staple theme of their production. Though they began with the bright colors and broken brushwork that signaled Impressionist modernity, there was no market for this kind of painting in the early 1890s.[37] Thus, they reverted to picturing the daughters of Boston's upper crust in interiors that recount the changeless tenor of Anglo-American life and the survival of the Brahmin social rituals of literature and tea (Fig. 14). Appropriately, Tarbell and Benson discarded the vibration and contrasts of Monet and Renoir for the timelessness of Vermeer and the Dutch "little masters." Their landscapes executed after the turn of the century appeal on the basis of their idealizations of young American women, often the artist's chil-

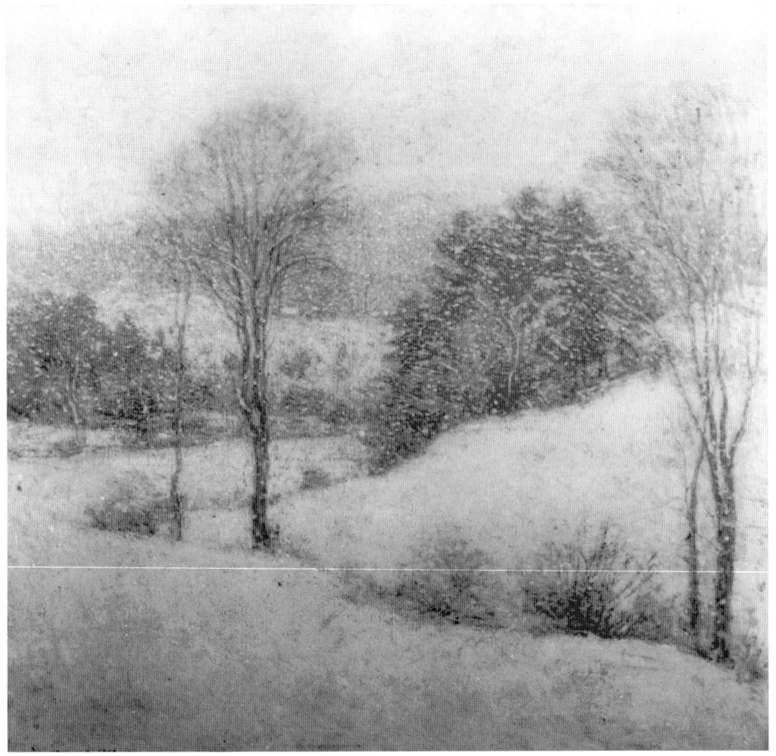

FIGURE 13 Willard Leroy Metcalf, *The White Veil*, 1909.
Oil on canvas. Museum of Art, Rhode Island School of Design,
gift of Mrs. Gustav Redeke.

dren. In harmonious tones of white, blue, and pink, these works exude health, fresh air, and sunshine. In short, their paintings reaffirm the supreme status of the bourgeois family, concretized in the innocent figures of girls in white, as the unassailable backbone of American society.

This domesticated Impressionism of the Boston school suggests a reconstitution of French Impressionism that actually redresses the first American criticisms of the French Impressionists. The unfavorable reception initially given to the French in America had to do with the social dilemmas of that historic moment, as these dilemmas collided with ideological mandates that American painters automatically and implicitly addressed in their works. The French, meanwhile, were not only oblivious to the cultural wars plaguing their potential American audience, but they were also indifferent to the needs and anxieties of the Anglo-American elite (which included the intelligentsia) as it adjusted to the vicissitudes of modernization. Rather, in the 1870s Monet and Renoir had

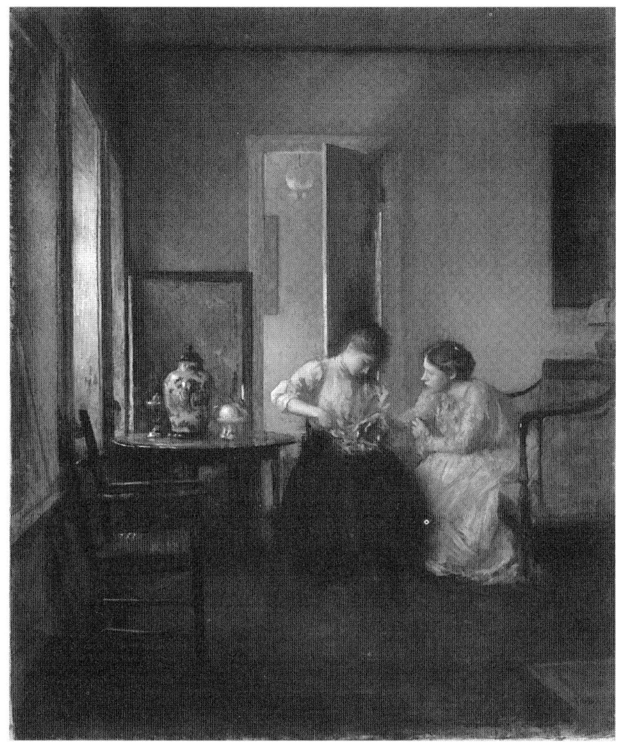

FIGURE 14 Edmund Charles Tarbell, *New England Interior.*
Oil on canvas. Museum of Fine Arts, Boston, gift of
Mrs. Eugene C. Epplinger.

uncritically celebrated everything the movers and shakers considered wrong with modern life. Writing in 1915 for *The New Republic*, the voice of American progressivism, Louis Weinberg summed up the case American critics had earlier made against Impressionism: indeed, the French had created the perfect expression of modernity, their writer opined, but who wanted it? They celebrated change and motion, flux and passing appearances, as well as the lowest common denominator of society. In such a dehumanized art form, in which men and women are treated as mere phenomena (Fig. 15), as blotches of paint, where were the big issues of human life, or even fundamental human passions? He suggested that what was wanted were standards and values, substance and stability, the significant and the enduring, all of which the Impressionists had sacrificed for the ephemeral.[38]

What Americans wanted in the 1890s is typified in the writings of one of the founding fathers of connoisseurship and art history, Bernard Berenson, whose

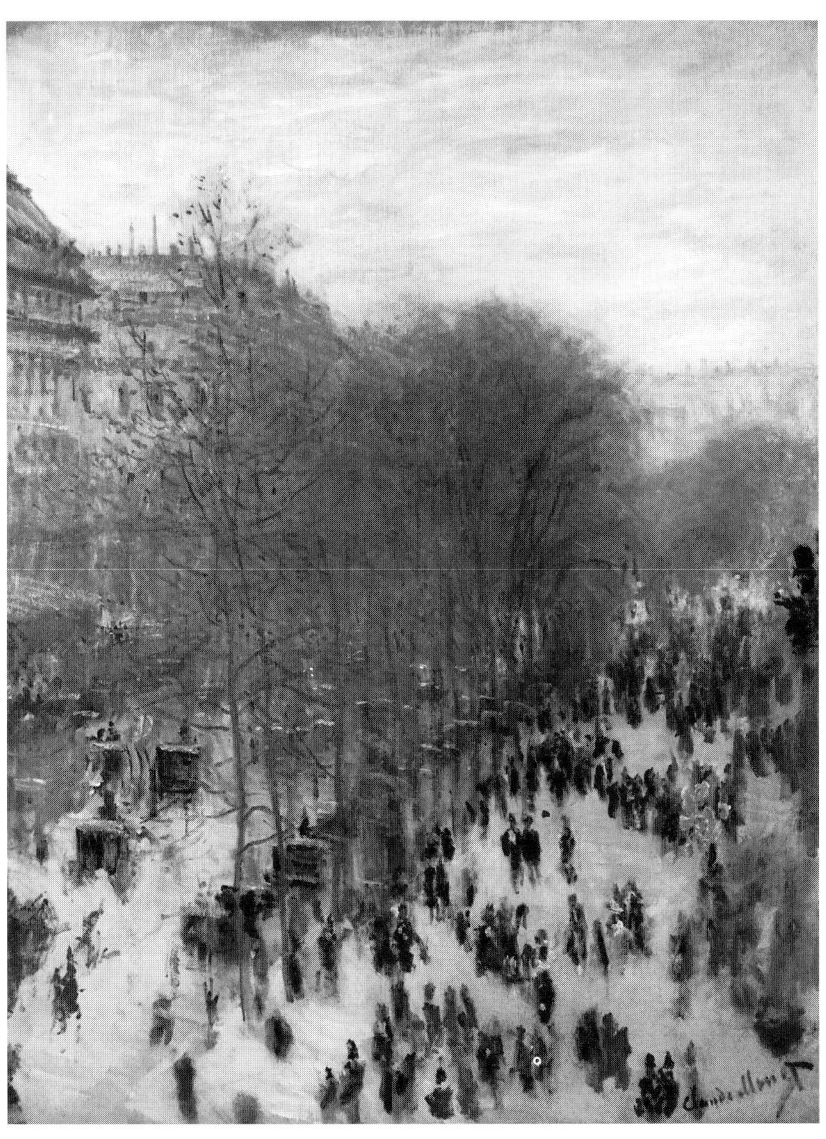

FIGURE 15 Claude Monet, *Boulevard des Capucines*, 1873-74. Oil on canvas. The Nelson-Atkins Museum of Art, purchased through the Kenneth A. and Helen F. Spencer Foundation Acqusition Fund.

attitudes were definitely shaped by this period of conflict and yearning for quietude. Berenson had been initiated into what we might call "the religion of art" at Harvard in the early 1880s, and his attitude toward the art object as a source of mystery and transcendence reflects the vaguely Asian sensibility that is shared by Twachtman's landscapes. Berenson wrote that, in the ideal aesthetic experience, "the spectator is at one with the work of art he is looking at...."

> He ceases to be his ordinary self, and the picture . . . or landscape . . . is no longer outside himself. The two become one entity; time and space are abolished. When he recovers workaday consciousness it is as if he had been initiated into illuminating, exalting, formative mysteries. In short, the aesthetic moment is a moment of mystic vision.[39]

The "ideated sensations that constitute the work of art," he said, "belong to a realm apart . . . a realm of contemplation, of 'emotion remembered in tranquility,'" so that its effect on the viewer is always "tempering and refining."[40] Sitting in his Florentine villa when he wrote this passage, Berenson was no doubt gazing reverently on a Quattrocento *Madonna and Child* and not an American landscape. But this anti-modernist mood of quietism is the same experience that Twachtman and others of his generation held out to their uneasy audience in the age of Darwin.

NOTES

1   The exhibition was held in May 1893 at the American Art Galleries in New York. See "Impressionism and Impressions," *The Collector* 4 (May 15, 1893): 2 13-14; and the *New York Daily Tribune* (May 15, 1893): 14. For other critical responses to this exhibition, see Dorothy Weir Young, *The Life and Letters of J. Alden Weir*, ed. with an introduction by Lawrence W. Chisolm (New Haven: Yale University Press, 1960), 178.

2   See, for example, Barbara Novak, "Introduction: Nature's Art," in *The Thyssen-Bornemisza Collection: Nineteenth-Century American Painting*, ed. by Barbara Novak and Elizabeth Garrity Ellis (New York: The Vendome Press, 1986), 39-40.

3   Richard Shiff, "The End of Impressionism," in *The New Painting: Impressionism, 1874-1886* exhibition catalogue (San Francisco and Washington, D. C.: The Fine Arts Museums of San Francisco, 1986), 71-74; Linda Nochlin, *Realism* (Harmondsworth, Middlesex: Penguin, 1978), 42-43, 53-54, and 143-45. Joel Isaacson, "Observation and Experiment in the Early Work of Monet," in *Aspects of Monet: A Symposium on the Artist's Life and Times*, ed. by John Rewald and Frances Weitzenhoffer (New York: Harry N. Abrams, Inc., 1984), 16-35; T. J. Clark, *The Painting of Modern Life: Paris in*

the Art of Manet and His Followers (New York: Knopf, 1984); Robert L. Herbert, *Impressionism: Art, Leisure, and Parisian Society* (New Haven and London: Yale University Press, 1988).

4 See Kathleen A. Pyne, "John Twachtman and the Therapeutic Landscape," in Deborah Chotner, Lisa N. Peters, and Kathleen A. Pyne, *John Twachtman: Connecticut Landscapes* (Washington, D C: National Gallery of Art, 1989), 49-69.

5 Monet to Durand-Ruel, July 28, 1885; quoted in translation by Frances Weitzenhoffer, "The Earliest American Collectors of Monet," in *Aspects of Monet,* 75. For the catalogue of Durand-Ruel's exhibition, see *Works in Oil and Pastel by the Impressionists of Paris* (New York: The American Art Association, 1886). Hans Huth, "Impressionism Comes to America," *Gazette des Beaux-Arts* 29 (April 1946): 225-52, provides the most detailed account of this venture, chronicles the earlier instances when a few Impressionist works (either singly or in small groups) were exhibited in the United States, and discusses a few early collectors of these French paintings. Earlier displays of French Impressionism consisted of the 1883 Foreign Exhibition at the International Exhibition for Art and Industry in Boston and the Art Loan Exhibition for the Statue of Liberty Pedestal Fund at the National Academy of Design in New York that same year.

6 J.[ohn] C. Van Dyke, "The Bartholdi Loan Collection," *The Studio* 2 (December 8, 1883): 262-63.

7 William Howe Downes, "Impressionism in Painting," *New England Magazine* 6 (July 1892): 600, recalled his thoughts on Manet's *Dead Christ with Angels* at its 1883 Boston exhibition.

8 "The Impressionists' Exhibition at the American Art Galleries," *The Art Interchange* 16 (April 24, 1886): 130.

9 "The French Impressionists," *The Critic* 5 (April 17, 1886): 195; for a reiteration of this position, see also "The Impressionists," *The Art Interchange* 29 (July 1892): 6; and W.[illiam] C. Brownell, *French Art: Classic and Contemporary Painting and Sculpture* (1892; New York: Charles Scribner's Sons, 190 1), 111-13. For a darker view of Degas's images as morally depraved, see "The Impressionists," *The Art Age* 3 (April 1886): 166.

10 "The Impressionists' Exhibition at the American Art Galleries," *The Art Interchange,* 130.

11 "The Impressionists," *The Art Interchange,* 6; and "The Impressionists," *The Art Age,* 165. "The Impressionists," *The Art Amateur* 30 (March 1894): 99, later reiterated the charge, albeit in a more positive vein, commenting that Renoir's depictions of Parisian low-life were comparable to Dickens's novels in offering "the most unvulgar pictures of vulgarity."

12 L. Lejeune, "The Impressionist School of Painting," *Lippincott's Magazine* 24 (December 1879): 725.

13 Pierce is quoted in James Turner, *Without God, Without Creed: The Origins of Unbelief in America* (Baltimore: The Johns Hopkins University Press, 1985), 206.

14 See Turner, 204-05; and D. H. Meyer, "American Intellectuals and the Victorian Crisis of Faith," *American Quarterly* 27 (December 1975): 584-603.

15 On these points, see Robert H. Wiebe's classic, *The Search for Order 1877-1920* (New York: Hill and Wang, 1967), especially 11-110; and Alan Trachtenberg, *The Incorporation of America: Culture and Society in the Gilded Age* (New York: Hill and Wang, 1982), especially 38-100.

16 Paul Avrich, *The Haymarket Tragedy* (Princeton, NJ: Princeton University Press, 1984), 197ff.; Trachtenberg, 88-89.

17 For biographies and ancestries of The Ten, see the *National Cyclopaedia of American Biography* (New York: James T. White and Company, 1900-56). On Koehler, see Rena Neumann Coen, *Painting and Sculpture in Minnesota: 1820-1914* (Minneapolis: Art Gallery, University of Minnesota, 1976), 108-09; and Patricia Hills, *The Painters' America: Rural and Urban Life, 1810-1910* (New York and Washington: Praeger Publishers, 1974), 123.

18 T. J. Clark, *The Painting of Modern Life: Paris in the Art of Manet and His Followers* (Princeton, NJ: Princeton University Press, 1984).

19 John Higham, *Strangers in the Land: Patterns of American Nativism, 1860-1925* (New Brunswick, NJ: Rutgers University Press, 1955), 135-38. Wiebe, 9 1-96, details the paranoia of the establishment and the general fears of a class war.

20 Wiebe, 134-42.

21 Brownell, 111. See also "The Impressionists," *The Art Age*, 165; William Howe Downes, "Boston Painters and Paintings," *Atlantic Monthly* 62 (December 1888): 782.

22 Henry Bacon, "Glimpses of Parisian Art," *Scribner's Monthly* 21 (December 1880): 170, wrote "Manet began the work of representing nature out of tune, as some men begin great social or political revolutions." On Renoir's "inharmonious accents in values" and "shrieking" color, see Edward Rudolf Garczanski, "Jugglery in Art," *The Forum* 1 (August 1886): 600.

23 Complaints about Monet's "violent" and "extremist" technique were ubiquitous in the press; for examples see "The Impressionists," *The Art Interchange*, 4-7; Young, 188, cites the *Boston Transcript* (1896) as treating French Impressionism as a painterly idiom of violence; "The Point of View," *Scribner's Magazine* 9 (May 1891): 657; "The Impressionists," *The Art Age*, 165; Theodore Child, "Impressionist Painting," *Art and Criticism: Monographs and Studies* (New York: Harper and Brothers, 1892), 164, characterized the French as reactionaries who promoted an unhealthy extremism; and Huth, 242, cites a *New York Herald* review of 1886 as castigating the Impressionists' "lustful rioting in color."

24 On the vogue for the Barbizon school in the 1880s and 1890s, see Peter Bermingham, *American Art in the Barbizon Mood* (Washington, DC: Smithsonian Institution Press, 1975); and Maureen O'Brien, *In Support of Liberty: European Paintings at the 1883 Pedestal Fund Art Loan Exhibition* (Southampton, New York: The Parrish Art Museum, 1986). On the collectors of Monet in the period following the 1886 Durand-Ruel exhibition, see Huth 225-52; and Frances Weitzenhoffer, "The Earliest American Collectors of Monet," in *Aspects of Monet: A Symposium on the Artist's Life and Times* ed. by John Rewald and Frances Weitzenhoffer (New York: Abrams, Inc., 1984), especially 79-82.

25 See, for example, Adeline Adams's review of the Armory Show, "The Secret of Life," *Art and Progress* 4 (April 1913): 925-32.

26 See, for example, Josiah Strong, *Our Country: Its Possible Future and Its Present Crisis*, ed. by Jurgen Herbst (1886; Cambridge, MA: The Belknap Press of Harvard University Press, 1963); also Wiebe, 38-39, 88-91, 96.

27 Peter B. Hales, *Silver Cities: The Photography of Urbanization, 1839-1915* (Philadelphia: Temple University Press, 1984), chapter two, has noted parallel strategies in the imagery of urban photographers of the 1890s.

28 Compare, for example, Hassam's *Rainy Day, Boston* (1885, Toledo Museum of Art) with Gustave Caillebotte's *Rainy Day, Paris Street* (1877, Art Institute of Chicago). The formal sources of Hassam's and Chase's views of New York are discussed in Jennifer A. Martin Bienenstock, "Childe Hassam's Early Boston Cityscapes," *Arts Magazine* 55 (November 1980): 168-7 1; Dianne H. Pilgrim, "The Revival of Pastels in Nineteenth-Century America: The Society of Painters in Pastel," *The American Art Journal* 10 (1978): 48; and William H. Gerdts, *American Impressionism* (New York: Abbeville Press, 1984), 48, 94-98.

29 See Hassam's *Washington Arch, Spring* (1890, Phillips Collection, Washington, DC).

30 On Central Park and its philosophy and function as a domain of the upper classes in the late nineteenth century, see Roy Rosenzweig and Elizabeth Blackmar, *The Park and the People: A History of Central Park* (Ithaca, New York: Cornell University Press, 1992), 238ff.

31 Higham, 139; Thomas Bender, *Toward an Urban Vision: Ideas and Institutions in Nineteenth-Century America* (Lexington: University Press of Kentucky, 1975), 105 and 197. On the transformation of the New England village, the threat posed to it by immigrants and industrialization, and the early twentieth-century preservation movements, see D. W. Meinig, "Symbolic Landscapes: Some Idealizations of American Communities," in *The Interpretation of Ordinary Landscapes: Geographical Essays*, ed. D. W. Meinig (New York and Oxford: Oxford University Press, 1979), 173-74; and David Lowenthal, "Age and Artifact: Dilemmas of Appreciation," in Meinig, 110ff.

32 Ulrich W. Hiesinger, *Impressionism in America: The Ten American Painters* (Munich: Prestel Verlag, 1991), 164-65.

33 Letter from Twachtman to Weir, dated April 6, 1885; typescripts of Twachtman's letters to Weir are owned by Ira Spanierman, New York.

34 Letter from Twachtman to Weir, dated April 6, 1885; on Twachtman's French paintings in the Whistlerian mode, see Pyne, 51.

35 For an enlargement of these points, see Pyne, 60-64.

36 By the end of his life, which came unexpectedly in 1902, Twachtman was separated from his wife and had gone briefly to Virginia to recover his health. Twachtman's letters written to Josephine Holley in Cos Cob during the years 1900-02 (archives of the Historical Society of the Town of Greenwich) record his suffering in these years. See also Eliot Clark, *John Twachtman* (New York: privately printed, 1924), 28 and 58; and Pyne, 65.

37 William H. Gerdts, *Masterworks of American Impressionism* (Einsiedeln: Eidolon AG; Thyssen-Bornemisza Foundation, 1990), 116, 159, notes that Tarbell's large exhibition piece *In the Orchard* (1891) never found a buyer, though its imagery and technique seemed calculated to build upon the success of his *Three Sisters: A Study in June Sunlight* (1890) which the year before had been purchased by the socially illustrious Mrs. J. Montgomery Sears of Boston.

38 Louis Weinberg, "Current Impressionism," *The New Republic* 2 (March 6, 1915): 124-25.

39 Bernard Berenson, *Aesthetics and History* (1948; Garden City, NY: Doubleday & Company, Inc., 1954), 93.

40 Berenson, 77. Interestingly, Berenson's response to "vulgarity" in Degas's female types, his washerwomen and ballet girls, was similar to that of the American critics surveyed above, in that he felt that Degas's aestheticizing of the "vulgar" in terms of tactile values and energized movement provided an interest lacked by the subject on its own; see 73.

American Impressionism
Goes West

CHARLES C. ELDREDGE

HENRY JAMES, whose artistic insights were as keen as his social ones, once observed: "It sounds like a paradox, but it is a very simple truth, that when to-day we look for 'American art' we find it mainly in Paris. When we find it out of Paris, we at least find a great deal of Paris in it."[1]

By 1893, when James's paradoxical truth was published, artists from the United States had been gravitating to the French capital for decades. In the years following the American Civil War and the Franco-Prussian War, the traffic peaked, and with it came an American "heyday at the Salons." As noted by Lois Fink, the "couple of hundred" Americans who had exhibited in the annual Paris exhibitions from 1800 to 1870 were followed by "more than a thousand" between 1872 and 1899.[2]

Many of the visitors were drawn to the new capital of art to study with the leading academicians whose works dominated the salons. Instruction from such painters as Jean-Léon Gérôme, Jules-Joseph Lefebvre, and Léon Bonnat helped shape the development of American students who flocked to their ateliers, as well as the taste of a generation of their compatriots. The academic tradition was, however, scarcely the sole source of inspiration for the growing community of American painters in Paris.

In April 1874, the First Impressionist Exhibition (as it came to be called in retrospect) opened in Paris. Although other artists had previously taken exception to the conventional standards of the annual juried salons and organized individual or collective "independent" exhibitions—most famously in the Salon des Refusés in 1863—none was to have a greater impact than this gathering, from which developed the series of eight exhibitions of the Impressionists that concluded in 1886. Although the exhibitors in these shows were many and varied, a core group quickly achieved prominence, including Claude Monet, Pierre-Auguste Renoir, Edgar Degas, and Camille Pissarro. In 1879 the Impressionists welcomed to their ranks the American artist, Mary Cassatt, protegée of Degas, who showed in all but one of the remaining group exhibitions.[3] She also served as an important advocate for the new movement among her compatriots and as a conduit for the conveyance of many Impressionist masterworks to American collections.

While Cassatt was unique in her alliance with the French masters, she was representative of the enthusiasm with which many Americans took to the new style, especially from 1886 when the dealer Durand-Ruel initiated frequent New York exhibitions—and sales—of French Impressionism. The vogue for painting *en plein air*, with its resulting freshness of color, led to the establishment of numerous summer art colonies at various vacation spots in the northeastern United States, and ultimately far beyond. Locales proximate to major art centers were especially popular, such as Shinnecock, Long Island, where William Merritt Chase directed this country's first summer school of *plein-air* painting from 1891 to 1902. There Chase tackled the effects of the moment, seeking to capture the immediacy of fleeting clouds and of evanescent coastal light. His objective—"I believe in single-sitting impressions"[4]—was inspired by the precedent of the French Impressionists, whose works he had admired in Europe and in American collections where they were increasingly well-represented. For him, as for many of the French Impressionists' early followers in the United States, considerations of technique eclipsed those of subject: "If one can paint a fence rail well," said Chase, "it is far better than an unsuccessful attempt at the most sublime scenery, for it is not what one does, but the way it is done."[5]

The American author Hamlin Garland was an early champion of the new style and penned an influential account of the French Impressionists' work; but he tempered his enthusiasm for the French manner with an admonition to his compatriots to apply the new technique to familiar subjects: "Each painter should paint his own surroundings. . . . art, to be vital, must be local in its subject."[6] Such concerns often led to a delight in familiar, indeed sometimes banal, landscape subjects like the fence rails of Shinnecock, or the weathered rural structures of southeastern Connecticut that were often depicted by what Childe Hassam called the "Cos Cob clapboard school."[7] It was a generational proclivity that provided the basis for Lewis Mumford's later characterization of the period as one of "intense absorption in the local and the regional."[8]

Hamlin Garland, however, the son of the Middle Border, was not content to let his impulse to the "local" rest in New York or New England with quaint, clapboard motifs. In decrying the habit of artistic expatriation, he celebrated the attractions of the American Midwest. For instance, "the Chicago artist, being denied certain picturesque aspects of seashore and mountain side, has a rare chance to develop unhackneyed themes in sky and plain. . . . The light floods the Kankakee marshes as well as the meadows and willows of Giverny. The Muscatatuck has its subtleties of color as well as L'Oise, and a little young haymaker on the banks of the Fox River is certainly as admirable . . . as a clumsy Brittany peasant in wooden shoes."[9]

As subjects, Illinois farm boys and Breton peasants might bear some resemblance; however, equally noteworthy are the obvious differences between the environment that spawned Impressionism and that to which Garland summoned attention. The humid valley of the Seine and the coastal settlements of Brittany and Normandy, favored by the French innovators, boasted qualities of light and atmosphere similar to many of the familiar art centers of the northeastern United States. The impression of a sunrise over Le Havre, for example, might not differ essentially from morning light's effect on New York Harbor or Peconic Bay. While Monet's style may vary in particulars from those of Chase, Twachtman, and other American Impressionists, those trans-Atlantic followers of the French masters at least shared inspiration from similar climatic environs. That similarity to the generative French ambience was not so easily recognized in the Midwest, however, Garland's acclamations notwithstanding. Also, it was even more remote from the Rocky Mountain West and beyond, arid regions so different from northwestern France. Yet, despite the differences in climate and topography, the Impressionist vogue eventually spread across the vast and varied American landscape, adapting readily to very different circumstances of light, scale, and color from those in its Seine valley birthplace.

The completion of the transcontinental railway in 1869, marked with the driving of the Golden Spike at Promontory Point, Utah, placed Americans in a new relationship to their distinctive western landscape. Out of the fascination with its dramatic scenery and its potential for development and fueled by a post-war prosperity and a nascent nationalism in the wake of sectional strife, a fledgling tourist boom began in the region. Visitors flocked to natural wonders, their migration facilitated by the railroads and encouraged by the popular press—and recorded by artists. Yosemite tourists provided subjects for the California painter Wilhelm Hahn in 1874 (*Yosemite Valley from Glacier Point*, California Historical Society, San Francisco), just as their eastern contemporaries did for Winslow Homer in the Catskills, at Long Branch, New Jersey, and other fashionable haunts.

Harper's New Monthly Magazine published a typical tale, of two sisters and their tourist dilemma:

"It is perfectly absurd for you to keep going to Europe in this way, summer after summer," remarked the Maiden, with the emphasis and exaggeration peculiar to younger sisters.

"We have only been twice," murmured the married sister, apologetically.

"But once is enough. That is, if you haven't seen Colorado, and the Yellowstone, and Tacoma, and Alaska, and Yosemite. Of course one wants to go once . . . if you want art, or history, or architecture, or associations, you must go to Europe for them. If you were going for the winter, or to study anything, I could understand it. But you are not. You are going only for the summer and for scenery. And you will go straight to that miserable little Tyrol—"

"Miserable little Tyrol!" exclaimed Mrs. Thayer, in dismay.

"—When you might go to the Yellowstone."[10]

Travelers had been flocking to Yellowstone in increasing numbers for more than a decade before Mrs. Thayer received her sisterly advice. The popular press added to the keen interest in the newly accessible area. For instance, *Scribner's* subscribers in 1872 read Richard Watson Gilder's acclamation of the region's "unexampled richness . . . as a field for the artist or the pleasure tourist. . . . Verily a colossal sort of junketing place!"[11] The place disproved skeptics of American claims to grandiosity, noted editor Gilder. He recalled the Yankee "boast of bigger lakes, larger rivers, louder thunder, and more forked lightning than any other country. If anyone doubt this hereafter, we shall refer them to the Yellowstone Park." The landscape's superlatives inspired a patriotic fervor akin to that of the Tyrol-averse younger sister in the *Harper's* tale: "Why," he concluded, "should we waste ourselves in unpatriotic wonderment over the gorge of the Tamina or the Via Mala, when Nature has furnished us with the Grand Canyon of the Yellowstone, in which the famed Swiss ravines would be but as a crevice or a wrinkle? Why run across the sea to stifle and sneeze over the ill odors of Solfaterra, when we can spoil our lungs or our trowsers to better effect, and on an incomparably larger scale, with the gigantic boiling springs and geysers of Montana? And why strain and stiffen our backs in staring up at Terni or the Schmadribach, which are but as side-jets and spray-flakes to the Titanic majesty of Wyoming Lower Falls?"[12]

A mountain man like Jim Bridger early recognized the special character of the Yellowstone's thermal region, which he described picturesquely as "a place where hell bubbles up."[13] Where hell once bubbled, tourists were shortly to congregate. Entrepreneurs were quick to capitalize on Yellowstone's remarkable attractions, particularly after it became a national park in 1872; from the late 1880s on, a tourist industry boomed in the area. The Northern Pacific Railroad widely advertised the park's attractions and delivered a growing horde of affluent

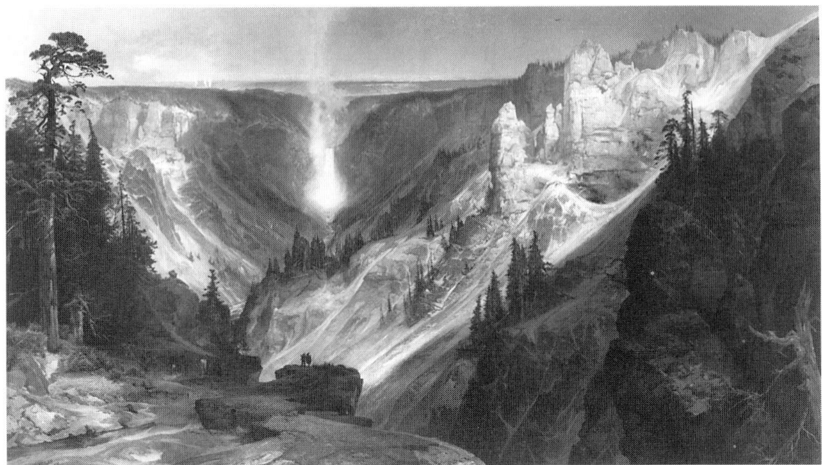

FIGURE 1 Thomas Moran, *The Grand Canyon of the Yellowstone*, 1872. Oil on canvas.
National Museum of American Art, Smithsonian Institution, lent by the
U.S. Department of the Interior, Office of the Secretary.

tourists to the coachmen and hotelkeepers of the park. The Yellowstone entrepreneurs succeeded, to the consternation of some of their visitors, such as Rudyard Kipling. "Today I am in the Yellowstone Park," he wrote in 1889, "and I wish I were dead." Kipling deplored the travel agent who "collects masses of Down-Easters from the New England States and elsewhere and hurls them across the Continent and into the Yellowstone Park on tour."[14]

An unprecedented legislative act of the U.S. Congress creating the first national park at Yellowstone in 1872 was inspired by the accounts of Ferdinand V. Hayden, leader of the survey expedition to the region in the previous year, and by the pictorial record of Thomas Moran, who had accompanied the Hayden group. Their reports, verbal and visual, astonished legislators and laymen alike, especially their descriptions of the Grand Canyon of the Yellowstone, which Hayden called "the greatest wonder of all."[15] In his enormous canvas of the subject (Fig. 1), Moran sought to convey his emotional response to the spectacle, conveyed paradoxically through what appeared to be geological specifics. He tried especially to capture the chromatic drama of the canyon, a challenge even for the artist who, as Hayden claimed, was "justly celebrated for his exquisite taste as a colorist." Awed by the canyon of the Yellowstone, Moran (according to Hayden) exclaimed, "with a sort of regretful enthusiasm, that these beautiful tints were beyond the reach of human art."[16]

Twenty-one years after his first memorable Yellowstone canvas, Moran re-

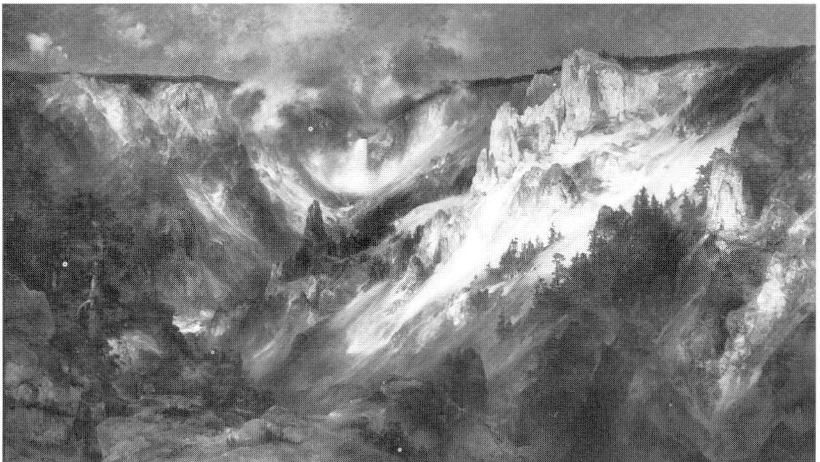

FIGURE 2 Thomas Moran, *The Grand Canyon of the Yellowstone*, 1893-1901. Oil on canvas. National Museum of American Art, Smithsonian Institution, gift of George D. Pratt.

turned to the subject in another monumental painting (Fig. 2). In this later example, the color was even more dramatically intense than in the initial panorama. The brushwork grew looser and, although it did not dissolve form in the Impressionist manner, it suggests Moran's susceptibility to the French vogue that by then was firmly implanted in America. Yet even Moran's more atmospheric reworking of the Yellowstone motif appears conventional when compared to the radical pictorial solutions that John Twachtman discovered at the park two years later.

In September 1895 the Impressionist Twachtman traveled from his Connecticut home to Yellowstone. This departure from his usual Eastern landscape inspirations was made at the request of his patron, William A. Wadsworth of Buffalo, New York, who provided the only direct commission in the artist's career. Traditionally, Twachtman's art is appreciated as the product of a deep attachment to home, a celebration of the familiar. But even a homebody needs release on occasion, as suggested in the artist's' jubilant report from the park: "This trip is like the outing of a city boy to the country for the first time. I was too long in one place. This scenery too is fine enough to shock any mind."[17] It was fine enough to inspire at least fourteen Twachtman paintings.

Moran's broad panoramas of the canyon lead the eye into the dramatic recesses, as if to illustrate the exclamations of early surveyors: "It is grand, gloomy, and terrible . . . an empire of shadows and turmoil."[18] By contrast, Twachtman's

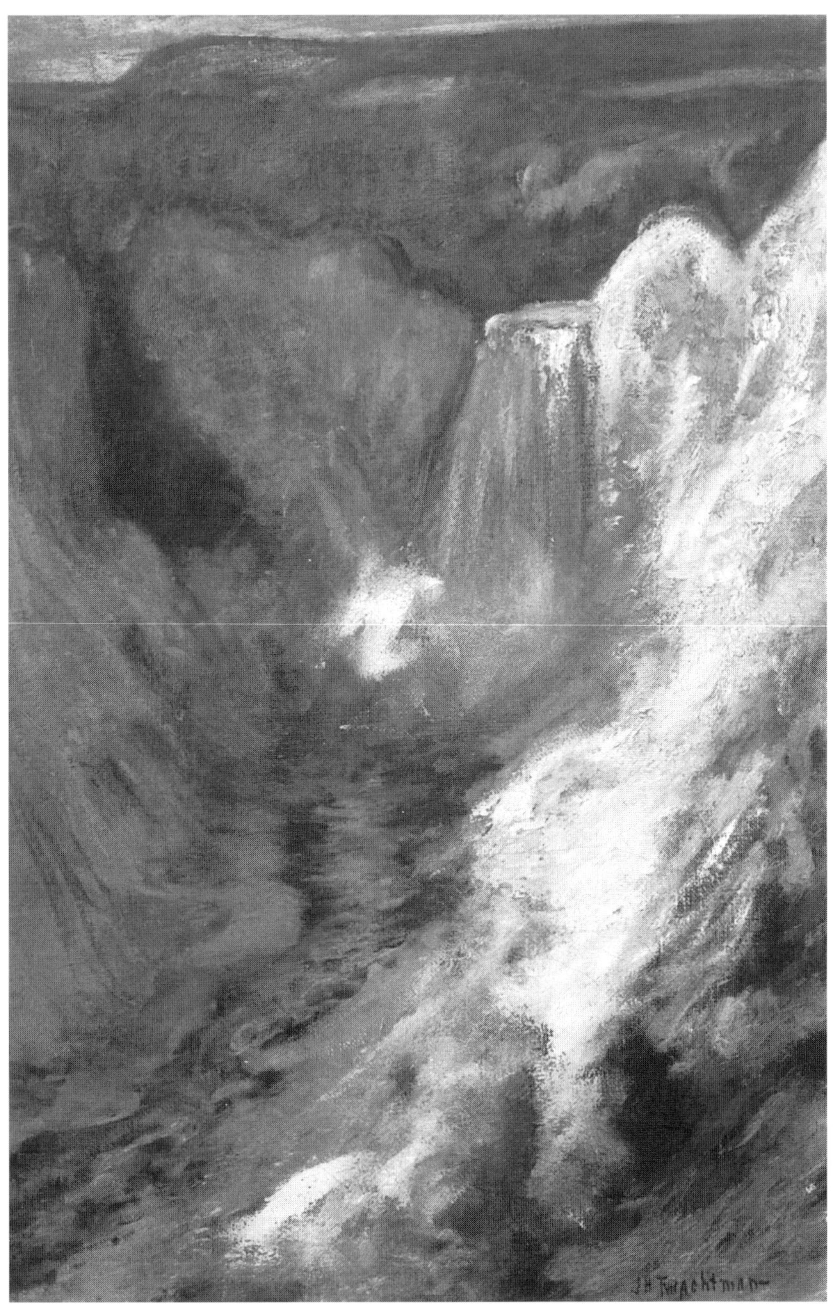

FIGURE 3 John Henry Twachtman, *Waterfall in Yellowstone*. Oil on canvas. Buffalo Bill Historical Center.

vertical compositions compress the image, adopting a view based on a fragment rather than the panorama (Fig. 3). The choice cancels the terror through a more intimate, telescopic vignette on the canyon and its distant cataract. With his pastel hues and daubs of pigment, the artist neutralizes the *terribilità* of Moran's subject; he is concerned with extracting from the subject design more than drama.

Many Yellowstone visitors exclaimed over the brilliant, multicolored formations, a geological spectrum of "all the colors of the land, sea, and sky," including that which gave the region its name.[19] For a colorist of Twachtman's gifts, the site provided an exceptional stimulus, which grew as the season changed. Snow scenes were always among the artist's favorite subjects, and his delight only increased after the landscape paled under winter's early mantle: "We have had several snow storms and the ground is white—the canyon looks more beautiful than ever."[20]

In the park's thermal region Twachtman painted two of the colorful hot pools that were favorite tourist destinations: Morning Glory Pool, which some visitors thought "worth a dozen [Old] Faithfuls," and the Emerald Pool, which, even "were there nothing else to see in the Park, . . . would be worth a journey."[21] Again, Twachtman's vantage was different from Moran's. Instead of a wide landscape overflowing with brilliantly tinted hot waters, as the earlier visitor painted at the Mammoth Hot Springs, the Impressionist approached his subject closely and fairly filled the canvas with its uptilted, rounded form. The steaming blue-green waters of Twachtman's *Emerald Pool* (Fig. 4) are described against the snow white ground in an elegant design akin to the curvilinear patterns, like art nouveau, that he often painted in winter views of the brook on his Connecticut farm. His contemporaries likened the Emerald Pool to "a thin goblet with Crème de Menthe, on the top [of which are] drop[ped] a few 'beads' of absinthe," and its mists rising in the cold air to "steam from a dirty laundry."[22] Needing no analogy by word or picture to other objects, natural or otherwise, Twachtman's fresh vision discovered in the Emerald Pool an abstract design. As described by Doreen Bolger, Twachtman's composition developed through his admiration of woodblock prints by the nineteenth-century Japanese master, Ando Hiroshige. The "actual landscape elements [in *Emerald Pool*] are virtually unrecognizable, viewed so close and painted so broadly that they are reduced to flat shapes bounded by sinuous lines."[23] Twachtman manages the unlikely transplant of Impressionist stroke and color, combined with a Japanese design sensibility, to realize some of the most remarkable nineteenth-century landscapes of the American West.

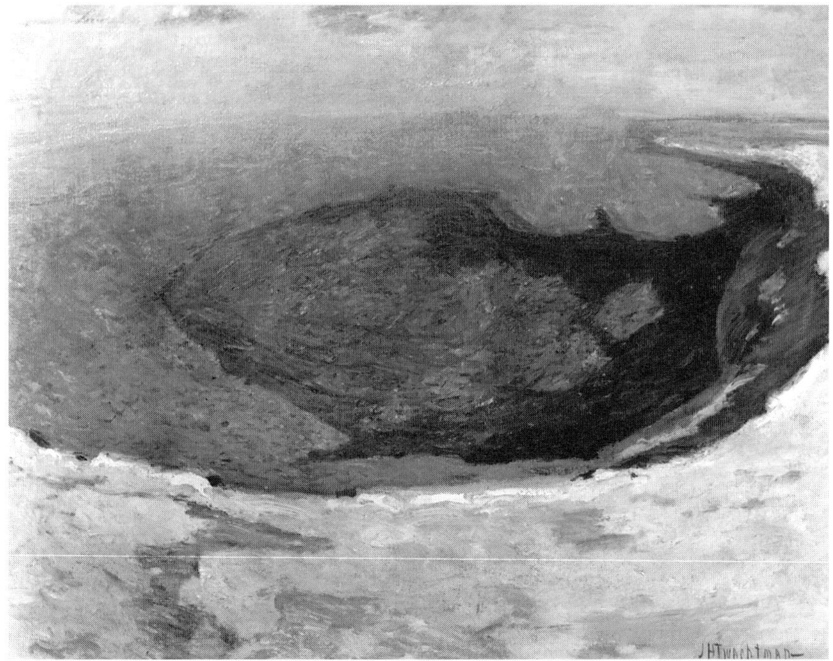

FIGURE 4 John Henry Twachtman, *Emerald Pool, Yellowstone*. Oil on canvas.
Wadsworth Atheneum, bequest of George A. Gay (by exchange)
and the Ellen Gallup Sumner and Mary Catlin Sumner Collection Fund.

Duncan Phillips, a dedicated champion of Twachtman's rarified landscapes, appreciated the uniqueness of his achievement. "Of course he did not try to copy or compete with the Rocky Mountains," Phillips acknowledged. "How frail would his lovely art have seemed if he had tried! His attitude was like that of the Oriental painters, who worshipped Nature by means of art. . . . It was the paradox of this art of Twachtman's that it grew out of the so-called 'impressionist' movement, which had stressed the evanescent appearance and physical aspects of the visible world, yet it matured into a lyricism which proclaimed its faith in the invisible and eternal."[24]

As Twachtman's vision transformed the familiar image of Yellowstone, so too did other painters re-discover the Western landscape through novel stylistic means. Thomas Moran was also an early depictor of the Grand Canyon of the Colorado, which he explored with Major John Wesley Powell's geological survey in 1873. As with the Hayden expedition to the Yellowstone, the Powell survey also led to a major Moran canvas, the monumental *Grand Canyon of the Col-*

orado, 1873-74, which likewise was purchased by act of Congress. Drawn with comparable precision, combining the effect of geological detail with awesome spectacle, the painting also contributed to rising public interest in the natural wonders of the West. In later years Moran revisited the Grand Canyon and painted numerous smaller canvases of the site. In these later treatments, as with those of the Yellowstone, atmospheric effects became newly important to the painter, suggesting another echo of the popular Impressionist technique. This looser manner, applied to Moran's modestly-sized, later Canyon pictures, effectively transformed the awesome chasm into congenial tourist ground. The change appeared to be the product of patronage, as style was put to the service of Moran's corporate sponsor, the Atchison, Topeka and Santa Fe Railroad, primary carrier to the Southwest. Geological record yielded to scenic view. Survey document became travel advertisement.

Moran and the railroad both profited from the interest in the Grand Canyon, which was further stimulated by a highly publicized visit from President Roosevelt in 1903. The Santa Fe railway had begun operating a branch line to the Canyon in 1901, and the year following the Presidential visit, in order to serve the swelling traffic, it opened a new hotel on the brink of the canyon, Fred Harvey's famed El Tovar Hotel. The hotel long remained the favored destination for the fortunate on a "Grand Tour" of the American West, providing them with private dining rooms, huge fireplaces, music and art rooms, a spacious ladies' lounge, an Indian Museum (Hopi House), and other comforts.

Of course, visitors to the Grand Canyon were not always so pampered. Photographer John Hillers worked at the canyon in 1872 in primitive, pre-Harvey conditions, recording its geological wonders. For the documentary purposes of his art, a clear focus and pictorial precision were at a premium. By 1911, however, when Alvin Langdon Coburn and Arthur Wesley Dow were both working with cameras at the canyon, the Impressionist-inspired haze of photographic pictorialism dominated; their interest was not in geological strata, stone chimneys, or erosion patterns, but in the general atmospheric effects of the site, which they captured with fogged impressions of light and shadow. In Dow's case, he later translated these blurred images into colorful plays of pigment brushed with a loose stroke indebted to Impressionism (Fig. 5).

The pilgrimage to the Grand Canyon provided many artists with their first introduction to the desert country of the Southwest. That terrain's harsh beauty did not easily nor readily figure in the country's expanding repertoire of regional landscape motifs, so remote was it from the common experience. Later, Georgia O'Keeffe often referred to the desert country of her beloved northern New Mexico as "the faraway." To earlier visitors the landscape of Arizona's

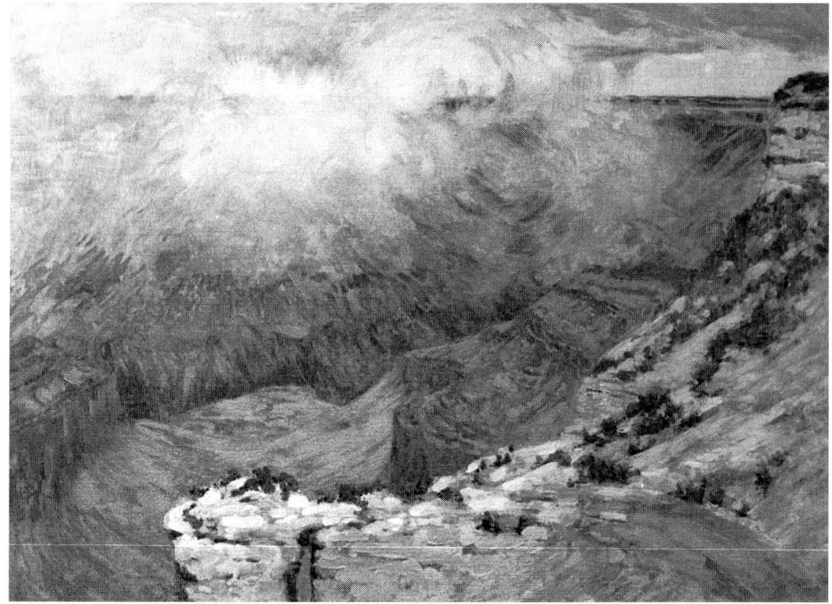

FIGURE 5 Arthur Wesley Dow, *Bright Angel Canyon*. Oil on canvas.
Ipswich Historical Society.

Painted Desert, Utah's salt flats, or California's Death Valley must have seemed even more foreign, faraway, and forbidding. The desert was defined, environmentally and in imagination, by its aridity. The clear air and hard light created a landscape of stark contrasts, of dramatic shadows and highlighted masses of dune or mesa. This was the regional image conveyed by Edward Weston's photographs of sandscapes in the 1930s or by Maynard Dixon's southwestern landscape paintings of the 1920s onward, works whose sleek, stylized forms transformed the subject into a Deco desert.

Yet, before their crystalline images captured the public imagination, other artists had resorted to more familiar techniques to capture their impressions of the arid country. So far from the Seine, from familiar scenes of farm and forest, the brilliant hues and broken stroke of Impressionist painting proved—perhaps unpredictably—adaptable to this most un-French of landscapes. Anna Hills arrived in California in 1912 and quickly became a leader of the fledgling Laguna Beach art colony, from which she explored a variety of California landscape motifs. The salubrious local conditions favored painting *en plein air*, even in the interior desert where Hills worked as early as 1915. There she caught the fleeting effects of light and shadow on sand and sage with means that owed much to Im-

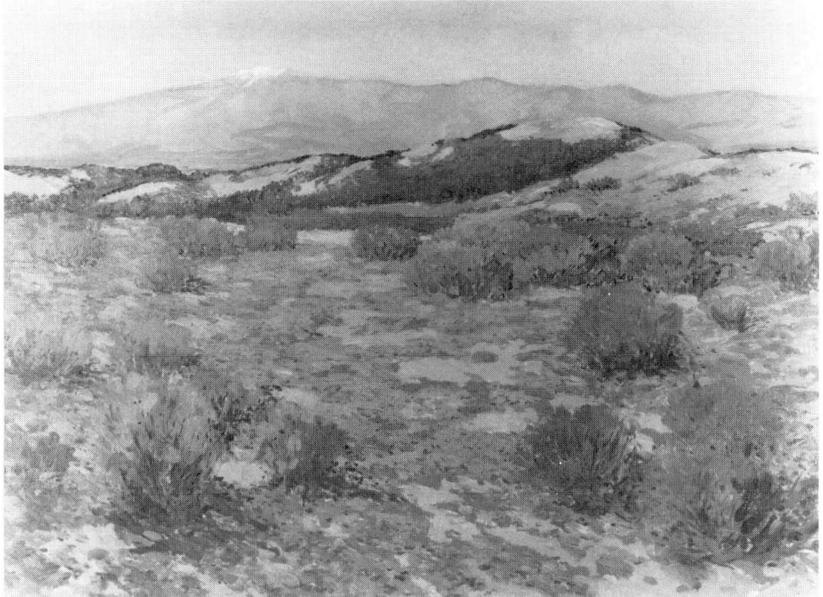

FIGURE 6 William A. Griffith, *Desert in Bloom*, 1926. Oil on canvas.
Spencer Museum of Art, University of Kansas.

pressionism. The interest in desert impressions was shared by other members of the Laguna colony, who insured the survival and vitality of the Impressionist style among California landscapists well beyond the First World War (Fig. 6).

A different desert drew Childe Hassam's attention. While working on a commission to decorate the Portland, Oregon, home of his friend and patron, Colonel C.E.S. Wood, Hassam made his initial western journey in 1904, serving effectively as Impressionism's John the Baptist in the Northwest. In the course of a return visit in 1908, his host introduced Hassam to the Harney desert, in Oregon's dry, southeastern quadrant. The area offered challenges rather different from the New England sites made familiar by his brush over the preceding several decades: in lieu of Cos Cob's weathered clapboards or Old Lyme's tidy church, there was little of man's mark in the emptiness of the vast desert; the sage-covered plateau was uninterrupted by graceful elms or ancient oaks, or colorful flowers of the sort Hassam painted in seaside gardens on the Isle of Shoals. In Harney County's "lean and stricken Land," as Wood once described it, Hassam discovered the peculiar effects of desert light and space; he was fascinated by what he described as "the limpid air, the stupendous skies, and the amethystine distances.”[25] Hassam's favorable response to the setting was doubtless shaped by his host's longtime affection for it. Again and again the poet-polymath Wood returned there

> to lose myself in immensity
> And to know my littleness.
> To lie in the lap of my mother
> And be comforted.
>
> A basaltic cliff, embroidered with lichens,
> Illumined by the sun, orange and yellow,
> The work of a great painter,
> Careless in the splash of his brush.[26]

During his summer's stay, Hassam was industrious with his brush, producing nearly forty paintings of the area's colorful effects (Fig. 7), impressionist designs whose "infallible instinct for decorative arrangement" was warmly received by Portland collectors.[27]

The favorable response to Hassam's style was a harbinger of even greater rewards heaped on the artist in the following decade. In the art exhibition at the Panama-Pacific International Exposition in San Francisco in 1915, Hassam was represented by thirty-eight paintings installed in a room of their own, a retrospective of his distinguished career; he was one of several contemporary Americans so honored—although no other was shown in such quantity—and nearly all of them were exemplars of Impressionism as adapted by native sons.[28] Such a large representation suggests that the Impressionist vogue was well established in California; yet such had not always been the case. At the turn of the century, as noted by William Gerdts, California painters had shown "little systematic interest in or absorption of Impressionist aesthetic," due to the late formation of the southern art centers and, in the more established San Francisco area, the domination of Arthur Mathews's conservative style of decoration, which "almost completely precluded an extensive investigation of Impressionism."[29]

It was a climate that was ready for conversion, and Hassam helped especially to stimulate that process. His contributions to the exposition were singled out for praise by influential critics, such as Christian Brinton. Among the Impressionists, he noted, "Only one American artist, Hassam, went as far as Monet, yet he has managed to individualize his brilliant, vibrant color appositions."[30] Hassam had brought to California this individual manner—and his charismatic personality—even before the Panama-Pacific Exposition. The previous year, he visited the San Francisco area and there produced a small group of landscapes, painted in the out of doors, that are distinguished by their heightened color, in-

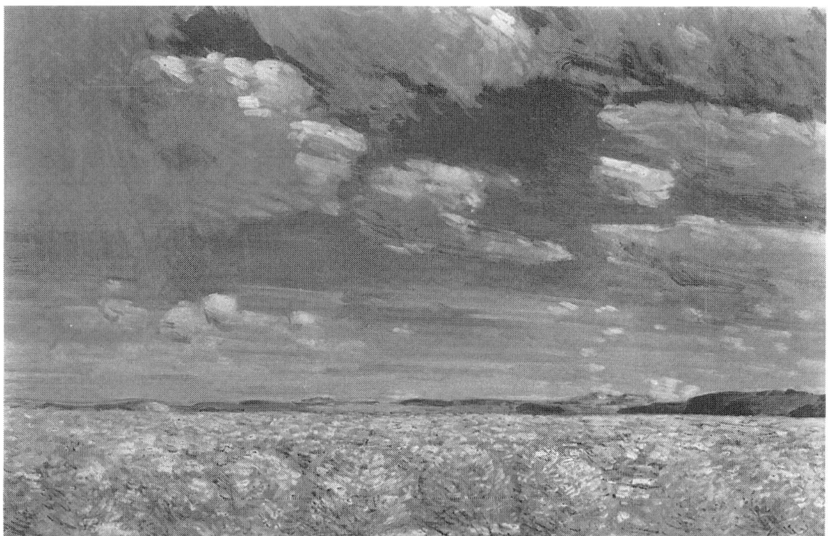

FIGURE 7 Frederick Childe Hassam, *Afternoon Sky, Harney Desert*, 1908. Oil on canvas. Portland Art Museum, gift of August Berg, Henrietta E. Failing, Winslow B. Ayer, William D. Wheelwright, I.N. Fleischner, estate of D.F. Thompson.

tense light, and sure handling. In *Hill of the Sun, San Anselmo* (Fig. 8), for instance, he produced a remarkable painting of an ordinary landscape, thickly applying his pigment to model the subject glowing with golden light. Critic John Caldwell, referring to the "almost abstract landscape forms and dissonant coloring" of the "unusual" San Anselmo view, speculated that Hassam was "experimenting in California in ways that he would not have done in New York." The painter seemed to be enjoying the liberating effects of distance, "feel[ing] the freedom to experiment that is the advantage of the provincial artist."[31]

While Hassam remained the outsider in California—albeit one unusually attuned to its peculiar environment—other artists resident in the state likewise responded in various innovative fashions to the local conditions. The Panama-Pacific International Exposition and its showcase for Impressionist painting was at once the catalyst and the consummation of this regional proclivity. During the early decades of this century—in burgeoning art colonies from Point Loma and Laguna to Carmel and Monterey Bay, and eventually even to the traditionalist art community of San Francisco—the French-born style took root in the American West, transforming the continental margin in a colorful blaze of light and color.

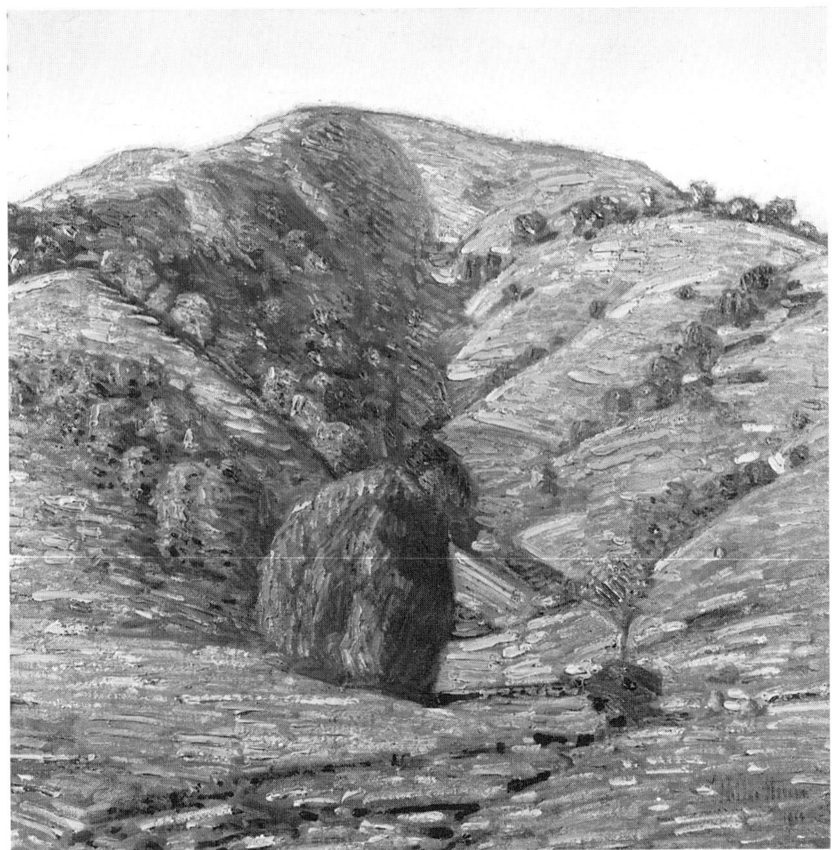

FIGURE 8 Frederick Childe Hassam, *Hill of the Sun, San Anselmo, California*, 1914. Oil on canvas. The Oakland Museum, gift of the Women's Board in honor of George W. Neubert.

The Panama-Pacific Exposition provided, by most accounts, the triumph of American Impressionism, both for the region and the country. In reviewing the highlights of that extravagant venture, Christian Brinton noted the dominance of the Impressionist aesthetic. He also observed with insight that by then—two decades after Henry James's quip—the French-born style had been naturalized in America. The critic warned that "it must not be assumed that American Impressionism and French Impressionism are identical. The American painter accepted the spirit, not the letter of the new doctrine. He adapted the division of tones to local taste and conditions and ultimately evolved a special or compromise technique."[32]

Across the United States, this acculturated style flourished, Impressionism effectively serving to familiarize the varied and unfamiliar landscape. Simultaneously, in its application to new terrains in new environmental conditions, style itself was reinvigorated, as American Impressionists experimented with western subjects with new freedom.

If the Panama-Pacific Exposition marked the nationalization of the Impressionist style, it also, in the retrospective honor accorded to its Old Masters, marked the movement's extent in time as well as space. As William Gerdts concluded, the exhibition "enshrined" the vogue: "Impressionism had become not only domesticated but historicized in America."[33] Through the elements of Impressionist style, which by 1915 enjoyed favor and fame, the landscape of "faraway," once a raw and daunting terrain, had been made reassuringly familiar. The West had been won, by painter's brush as well as gun.

I am very grateful to the General Research Fund of the University of Kansas, which generously supported the preparation of this study, and to my research assistant, Sarah Burt, for her indefatigable efforts and important contributions to this venture.

NOTES

1   Henry James, "John S. Sargent," in *The Painter's Eye: Notes and Essays on the Pictorial Arts by Henry James*, ed. John L. Sweeney (London: Rupert Hart-Davis, 1956), 216; reprint of essay published in *Picture and Text*, 1893, that being an emendation of an essay that first appeared in *Harper's Magazine*, October 1887.

2   Lois Marie Fink, *American Art in the Nineteenth-Century Paris Salons* (Washington: National Museum of American Art, and Cambridge: Cambridge University Press, 1990), 113.

3   Cassatt showed with the Impressionists in 1879, 1880, 1881, and again in the final exhibition in 1886. For an account of the eight exhibitions, see Charles S. Moffett *et al.*, *The New Painting: Impressionism 1874-1886* (San Francisco: The Fine Arts Museums of San Francisco, 1986).

4   William Merritt Chase, "Address of Mr. William M. Chase Before the Buffalo Fine Arts Academy, January 28, 1890," *The Studio* 5:13 (March 1, 1890): 124.

5   Quoted in Ronald G. Pisano, *Summer Afternoons: Landscape Paintings of William Merritt Chase* (Boston: Little, Brown and Company, 1993), 13.

6   Hamlin Garland, "Impressionism," *Crumbling Idols* (1894; Cambridge: Harvard University Press, 1960), 103.

7   The term was used by Childe Hassam to describe the artistic coterie that included his friends Weir, Twachtman, and Robinson. See Charles C. Eldredge, "Connecticut Im-

pressionists: The Spirit of Place," *Art in America* 62:5 (September-October 1974): 84-90.

8   Lewis Mumford, *The Golden Day* (Boston: Beacon Press, 1957), xxvii.

9   Hamlin Garland, Introduction to the Palette and Cosmopolitan Art Clubs exhibition, Chicago, 1895; quoted in William H. Gerdts, *American Impressionism* (Seattle: Henry Art Gallery, University of Washington, 1980), 104.

10   Alice Wellington Rollins, "The Three Tetons," *Harper's New Monthly Magazine* (May 1887): 869.

11   Richard Watson Gilder, "Culture and Progress," *Scribner's* (May 1872): 120.

12   Gilder, "Nature and Progress," 120-121.

13   James Bridger, quoted in Henry T. Finck, "Yellowstone Park as a Summer Resort," *The Nation* (September 27, 1900): 248.

14   Kipling, quoted in Schullery, ed. *Old Yellowstone Days*, 87.

15   F. V. Hayden, "The Wonders of the West: More About the Yellowstone," *Scribner's Monthly* (February 1872): 392.

16   Hayden, "The Wonders of the West," 392.

17   Twachtman to William A. Wadsworth, [Geneseo, NY], September 22, 1895; The Wadsworth Family Papers, College Libraries, State University of New York College of Arts and Sciences at Geneseo. Courtesy of Lisa Peters, John Twachtman Catalogue Raisonné, Ira Spanierman Gallery, New York, N.Y.

18   Lt. Gustavus C. Doane (1870), quoted in National Parkways, *A Photographic and Comprehensive Guide to Yellowstone National Park* (Casper, WY: Worldwide Research and Publishing Company, 1976), 41.

19   T. Dewitt Talmadge, quoted in Hiram Martin Chittenden, *The Yellowstone National Park, Historical and Descriptive* (Cincinnati: Stewart & Kidd Co., 1917), 302.

20   Twachtman to Wadsworth, *op. cit.*

21   Rollins, "The Three Tetons," 887; Warner, quoted in Schullery, 160.

22   J. Sanford Saltus, *A Week in the Yellowstone* (1895), quoted in Lee H. Whittlesey, *Yellowstone Place Names* (Helena: Montana Historical Press, 1988), 53; Warner, quoted in Schullery, 160.

23   Doreen Bolger, "American Artists and the Japanese Print: J. Alden Weir, Theodore Robinson, and John H. Twachtman," in *American Art Around 1900: Lectures in Memory of Daniel Fraad*, Doreen Bolger and Nicolai Cikovsky, Jr., eds., *Studies in the History of Art* 37 (Washington. DC: National Gallery of Art, 1990), 20.

24   Duncan Phillips, "Twachtman—An Appreciation," *International Studio* 66 (February 1919): cvi. More recently, Kathleen A. Pyne has similarly distinguished between the optical effects of Impressionism and the spiritual quality of Twachtman's late works, in which he invented "an idiosyncratic form of the Buddhist mind landscape." With reference to Twachtman's scenes of Connecticut brooks and waterfalls, Pyne drew parallels to Buddhism and Taoism; in both, water imagery figures prominently, as symbol for understanding of the world, as metaphor for transcendence. In his distinctive treatment of aquatic motifs—whether Connecticut brooks or Yellowstone's

thermal pools—the artist was not simply capturing fleeting moments of color and atmosphere. "In insisting on the experience of merging with this slow, nearly imperceptible movement in nature, in yielding the boundaries of the self and entering this fluid state of being, Twachtman found comfort and security in his submergence in this universal mother." (Deborah Chotner, Lisa N. Peters and Kathleen A. Pyne, *John Twachtman: Connecticut Landscapes* (Washington: National Gallery of Art, 1989), 62.)

25 "The Poet in the Desert," in *Collected Poems of Charles Erskine Wood*, ed. Sara Bard Field (New York: Vanguard Press, 1949), 157; Hassam, quoted in Adeline Adams, *Childe Hassam* (New York: American Academy of Arts and Letters, 1938), 104.

26 "The Poet in the Desert," 158.

27 Charles Erskine Scott Wood, "The Exhibition of Paintings of Eastern Oregon by Childe Hassam," *Pacific Monthly* 21, no. 2 (February 1909): 144. Wood here mentions Hassam's prolific output, remembering 27 canvases and 10 to 12 smaller panels produced in the summer of 1908.

28 Other one-man rooms were devoted to Edmund Tarbell, Edward Redfield, Frank Duveneck, William Merritt Chase, Gari Melchers and John Singer Sargent; similar recognition was given to three deceased artists, James McNeill Whistler, John Twachtman, and William Keith of California.

29 William H. Gerdts, *American Impressionism* (Seattle: Henry Art Gallery, University of Washington, 1980), 106.

30 Christian Brinton, *Impressions of the Art at the Panama-Pacific International Exposition, with a Chapter on the San Diego Exposition and an Introductory Essay on the Modern Spirit in Contemporary Painting* (New York: John Lane Co., 1916), 15-16.

31 John Caldwell, "California Impressionism: A Critical Essay," in *Impressionism, The California View: Paintings 1890-1930* (Oakland, CA: Oakland Museum 1981). n.p.

32 Brinton, 16.

33 William H. Gerdts, *American Impressionism* (New York: Abbevillle, 1984), 301, 306.

CONTRIBUTORS

SARAH BURNS (Ph.D. University of Illinois at Urbana-Champaign) is professor of the history of art in the Henry Radford Hope School of Fine Arts at Indiana University. In *Pastoral Inventions: Rural Life in Nineteenth-Century American Art and Culture* (Temple Press 1989) she examined the intersection of high art and popular imagery in such subjects as the barefoot boy, the noble yeoman, and the country bumpkin. She explores the other, more privileged side of American culture in her book on the modernization of the artist in America's Gilded Age (Yale University Press 1996).

CHARLES C. ELDREDGE (Ph.D. University of Minnesota) is the Hall Distinguished Professor of American Art at the University of Kansas. As former director of the National Museum of American Art, he curated numerous exhibitions and authored their accompanying catalogues, including the groundbreaking *American Imagination and Symbolist Painting* (1979). His most recent book on the art of Georgia O'Keeffe was published in conjunction with a major exhibition, Georgia O'Keeffe: American and Modern (Yale University Press 1993).

NANCY MATTHEWS (Ph.D. New York University) is the Eugénie Predergast Curator at the Williams College Museum of Art. In 1990 she curated and wrote the catalogue for an exhibition held at the Whitney Museum on the art of Maurice Pendergast. She has written two books on Mary Cassatt and several studies on the women in the Impressionist circle.

KATHLEEN PYNE (Ph.D. University of Michigan) is associate professor of the history of art at the University of Notre Dame. A specialist on *fin-de-siècle* American art, she has contributed essays to *John Twachtman: Connecticut Landscapes* (National Gallery of Art 1989) and *American Icons* (Getty Center 1992). She further examines American Impressionism, modernism, and Darwinism in *Art and the Higher Life: Painting and Evolutionary Thought in Late Nineteenth-Century America* (University of Texas Press 1996).

JANICE SIMON (Ph.D. University of Michigan) is associate professor of the history of art at the Lamar Dodd School of Art at the University of Georgia. Intrigued with the role of art periodicals in nineteenth-century American culture, she has written studies on *The Crayon* and *The Aldine*. A forthcoming book examines the forest interior view as a significant type in American landscape art and culture from the threshold imagery of Durand and Whittredge to the mythic forests created by Charles Burchfield and Walt Disney.